Instructor's Manual to Accompany

Research Design and Methods
A Process Approach

Fourth Edition

Kenneth S. Bordens
Bruce B. Abbott
Indiana University–Purdue University, Fort Wayne

Mayfield Publishing Company
Mountain View, California
London • Toronto

CONTENTS

Copyright © 1999, 1996, 1991 by Mayfield Publishing Company

International Standard Book Number: 0-7674-0696-6

Manufactured in the United States of America
10   9   8   7   6   5   4   3   2   1

Mayfield Publishing Company
1280 Villa Street
Mountain View, California 94041

PREFACE

Creating lectures, demonstrations, and laboratory exercises for the research methods course can demand a considerable amount of your time and energies, especially when adopting a new text. Even if you have taught the research methods course before, keeping the course fresh and current may require significant revision and reorganization of lectures, lab projects, and other in-class activities.

We created an instructor's manual for the second edition of our text to ease the burden the research methods course places on an instructor. We have continued this practice by offering this instructor's manual to accompany the fourth edition of *Research Design and Methods: A Process Approach*. As before, the manual includes sections designed to help you identify the important ideas and facts presented in each chapter of the text, suggestions for topics to cover in your lectures, and class activities for both laboratory and nonlaboratory settings.

Each chapter begins with a set of "Key Questions to Consider" and a chapter outline. A list of the "Key Terms" (those terms boldfaced in the text and defined in the glossary) follows the chapter outline. Next is a section titled "Chapter Goals," which indicates our intentions for the chapter, along with a list of suggested topics to be covered in your class.

For added convenience, the key questions and chapter outlines are included on a computer disk in ASCII files. You can retrieve these files with any word processor that can import ASCII files (DOS text files) such as WordPerfect. You can modify them as you wish for use in your class. For example, you could use a chapter outline as a framework for your lecture notes; just add your notes under the appropriate headings. You could print out and reproduce the key questions for distribution to your students who do not purchase the study guide available with our text.

The final section in the manual presents ideas for activities that you and your students can do in the classroom, laboratory, or in some cases, elsewhere. We and our colleagues have used these activities with our classes and they work quite well (or at least they did work, at least *once*!). You can use them as provided or modify them as you see fit. Give them a try, and perhaps let us know how things went. Better yet, if you have suggestions for activities that *you* find work, let us know about them. We would like to include them in future editions of this manual.

Changes for the Fourth Edition

The instructor's manual for the fourth edition is organized in the same way as the instructor's manual for the previous edition. There are some changes, however, that have been made. First, we have expanded the list of key questions to consider for most of the chapters, as we did for the student study guide. We have also expanded many of the items in the "Chapter Goals" sections to include more material and new material added to the text. We have also included some new "Ideas for Class Activities" centering on the Internet. For Chapter 2 we have included an activity that has students use the *PsycLit* tutorial at the APA Web site. For Chapter 3 there is an activity that has students use a research methods tutorial provided by Cornell University. Finally, for Chapter 13 we have provided a list of Web sites that have APA writing guides. You can have your students visit one or more of those sites to learn more about APA writing style.

We hope that you find this manual useful and that it makes it easier for you to teach this challenging course. Please feel free to contact us if you have any questions or feedback about this manual. We would also appreciate hearing from you about some of the things you are doing in class that you have found to be successful. You might find them included in future editions of this manual (with your permission and full credit, of course). You can reach us by e-mail at the following addresses:

<bordens@ipfw.edu>
<abbott@ipfw.edu>

We hope to hear from you.

Ken Bordens and Bruce Abbott

LABSTAT

LabStat is an integrated package of statistical programs providing many of the most commonly used descriptive and inferential statistics. Geared for student use, LabStat is simple to use, yet powerful enough to handle the analysis of data from most student projects, from simple correlational designs to three-factor mixed ANOVAs. Convenient data entry and editing are provided by a spreadsheet entry format, and data analyses are specified via menu selections and form-completion formats. LabStat runs on IBM and IBM-compatible personal computers and is available free of charge to adopters of the text. You can download the files needed to run LabStat on your computer along with the LabStat documentation from our Web site <http://www.ipfw.edu/nf1/bordens/web/rdm4/index1.htm>. Key features include the following:

- Accommodates up to 36 variables or treatments.
- Accommodates up to 120 scores per variable or treatment.
- Logarithmic, inverse, arcsin, and linear data transformations.
- Correlation, regression, and scatterplot.
- Inferential statistics include:
    Single-sample t test
    Independent samples t test
    Correlated samples t test
    One-way ANOVA
    Repeated measures ANOVA
    Two-factor ANOVA (between, within, mixed)
    Three-factor ANOVA (between, within, mixed)
    Mann–Whitney U test

TRANSPARENCIES

For each chapter we have prepared a set of transparencies. These transparencies are either enlarged reproductions of figures or tables in the text or plates that summarize key points made in a chapter. A few examples from selected chapters are listed here:

Chapter 1:   The defining qualities of scientific explanation, the major characteristics of the scientific method, circular explanations, the research process

Chapter 3:   The characteristics of experimental research, the characteristics of correlational research, strengths and limitations of experimental and correlational research

Chapter 12:   The relationship between samples and populations given the null hypothesis is true or false, one-tailed versus two-tailed tests, partitioning variance, the relationship between main effects and interactions

Chapter 13:   Setting up an APA-style manuscript, summary of the contents of each section of an APA-style manuscript, general-to-specific organization of an introduction, specific-to-general organization of a discussion section, drawing graphs correctly, examples of reference citations

These transparencies will make it easier for students to grasp the central themes and material in each chapter. You can use the transparencies to organize your lectures and to tie your lectures to the material in the text.

CHAPTER 1

EXPLAINING BEHAVIOR

KEY QUESTIONS TO CONSIDER

- What are the two steps suggested by Cialdini (1994) for exploring the causes for behavior and how do they relate to explaining behavior?
- What are the main characteristics of a scientific explanation?
- How do scientific and commonsense explanations differ?
- How do belief-based and scientific explanations differ?
- What kinds of questions do scientists refrain from investigating?
- How can faulty inference invalidate a scientific explanation?
- What are pseudoexplanations and how do you avoid them?
- What are the defining characteristics and weaknesses of the method of authority and rational method?
- What is the scientific method and why is it preferred in science?
- What is the difference between a method and a technique?
- How do basic and applied research differ? How are they similar?
- How are the steps of the scientific method applied to answering research questions?
- What are the steps of the research process and what important decisions must be made at each step?
- How do decisions made early in the research process affect decisions made and conclusions drawn later in the process?

CHAPTER OUTLINE

KEY TERMS

Research	Rational method
Scientific explanation	Scientific method
Parsimonious explanation	Variable
Commonsense explanation	Hypothesis
Belief-based explanation	Basic research
Pseudoexplanation	Applied research
Circular explanation or tautology	Deductive reasoning
Method of authority	Pilot study

CHAPTER GOALS

The purpose of Chapter 1 is to introduce your students to the foundations of science and scientific research. The chapter focuses on the differences between scientific and nonscientific explanations (commonsense and belief-based) and the different methods of acquiring knowledge. Students should come away with a sense that the goal of psychology is to uncover scientific explanations for behavioral phenomena and that the scientific method is the preferred method of finding such explanations. During class periods you might focus your lectures on the following:

- The defining characteristics of scientific explanations.
- How scientific explanations differ from commonsense and belief-based explanations.
- Why scientific explanations are preferred over commonsense and belief-based explanations.
- How faulty inference processes and pseudoexplanations affect the validity of scientific explanations.
- The defining characteristics of the method of authority, rational method, and scientific method.
- The problems associated with using the method of authority or the rational method as the principal method of inquiry.
- The characteristics of the scientific method and why it is preferred over other methods of inquiry for the acquisition of scientific knowledge.
- The distinction and overlap between basic and applied research.
- The steps involved in the research process.

IDEAS FOR CLASS ACTIVITIES

Research Findings in the Popular Press

Chapter 1 develops the idea that science (generally) and the research process (specifically) are the best ways to acquire knowledge. However, students may remain unconvinced, especially those who don't see a research future for themselves. You can underscore the importance of understanding scientific explanations and research by having students read and evaluate articles from popular magazines (for example, *Time, Newsweek,* or *Psychology Today*). Students could look for the following:

    a. How many articles in a particular issue cite scientific research to support the main ideas in the article. This gives students a sense of just how prevalent research is in their lives.

    b. After choosing one or two articles to evaluate, students should note what kinds of data were reported in the article. For example, what statistics were reported (averages, frequency counts, standard deviations, and so on)? This will get students used to looking for relevant data reported in articles and help them to identify how research data are reported. This serves as a good lead-in for reading a scientific article (covered in Chapter 2).

    c. Have students evaluate whether the author's conclusions follow logically from the data reported. This will introduce students to reading articles critically.

    d. Point out that sources such as *Time* and *Newsweek* are secondary sources and if they are used as the prime source of information, then the method of authority is being used. Ask students to outline any dangers they see in using popular sources as primary sources of information. Students could focus on the idea that research results often are reported selectively in such publications and details of the methods used to acquire the data often are not given.

Identifying the Method of Inquiry

In Chapter 1 the issue of bystander intervention was used to introduce students to the application of research to a real-world problem. You can reinforce this point by using another example, perhaps from your own research area or a current event, to show how popular, commonsense explanations fail to explain behavior adequately. Popular magazines and newspapers are good sources for current events that can be discussed in the light of the scientific method. Encourage your students to peruse the newspaper daily for examples of behavior that have been explained in commonsense ways. Have them point out possible flaws in the explanations given for the behavioral event and suggest ways that a scientific explanation can be developed.

Applying the Scientific Method

Chapter 1 opens with a description of the case of Vanessa Moretti, the little girl whom nobody stopped to help. Later in the chapter the "bystander effect" is used to illustrate how various types of explanations may fail to explain such an effect. You can extend the example in the book by having students find current issues (e.g., another case of bystander nonintervention or a political question) and try to follow the steps of the scientific method to uncover answers to some of the questions surrounding the issue chosen. Students should identify where they found their initial information on the issue, develop a testable research hypothesis, and speculate on how they would go about using the scientific method to evaluate their hypothesis. Students could also contrast using the scientific method with using the other methods of inquiry discussed in Chapter 1.

Class Discussion

Come to class with a controversial question to pose to students. For example, you could ask students if early infant day care is harmful to children, or whether heredity or environment is more important in shaping behavior. Have students give their opinions, and perhaps write them on the board as you go. Discuss whether their opinions are based on common sense, religious belief, or some other source. Next, ask the class how the question being evaluated could be evaluated scientifically. Use this opportunity to introduce your students to the characteristics of the scientific method and the research process. Have students speculate about how they would evaluate the question using the scientific method.

The Scientific Method in Action

Show the film *The Case of the Frozen Addict* to your class. The film is a 1996 show from the *Nova* series on PBS. It is available from the Indiana University Film Rental Library (EC2288, VH). You can contact them by telephone: Outside Indiana, 1-800-552-8620; within Indiana, 1-800-942-0481. This film, although intended to explore the biochemistry of drug action, provides an excellent overview of how science works. Have your class specifically look for how the scientists shown in the film developed ideas and hypotheses, applied the scientific method, and carried out research. Also, there are a couple of segments where serendipity plays a key role in unraveling the puzzle posed to the scientist (for example, having some of the original lab equipment available and one researcher having read an article in a relatively obscure journal). After viewing the film, discuss how the scientific method was used to "crack the case," and how the research process proceeded throughout the case.

CHAPTER 2

DEVELOPING IDEAS FOR RESEARCH

KEY QUESTIONS TO CONSIDER

- How do you use unsystematic and systematic observation to help develop research ideas?
- What makes a research question answerable and important?
- How can a thorough review of the literature help you develop good research questions?
- What is the difference between a primary and secondary source and how should each be used?
- What are the differences between nonrefereed and refereed journal articles?
- How do the major sources of research information differ?
- What are *PsycLit* and the *Psychological Abstracts* used for?
- How can you narrow or broaden a computerized literature search?
- What are the advantages and disadvantages of computer literature searches?
- Why is it important to read a research report critically?
- What rules should you follow when reading a research report critically?
- What should you look for in each section of an APA-style research report?

CHAPTER OUTLINE

Sources of Research Ideas
    Unsystematic Observation
    Systematic Observation
    Theory
    The Need to Solve Practical Problems
Developing Good Research Questions
    Asking Answerable Questions
    Asking the Right Questions
    Asking Important Questions
Reviewing the Literature
Sources of Research Information
    Primary Versus Secondary Sources
    Where to Find Research
        Books
        Scientific Journals
        Conventions and Professional Meetings
        Other Sources of Research Information
Performing Library Research
    The Basic Strategy
    Research Tools
    Using *PsycLit*
        Conducting a *PsycLit* Search
        Narrowing Your Search
        A Note of Caution About Using *PsycLit*
        Other Computerized Databases

KEY TERMS

Theory	Nonrefereed journal
Empirical question	Paper sessions
Operational definition	Personal communications
Literature review	*Psychological Abstracts*
Primary source	*PsycLit*
Secondary source	*Thesaurus of Psychological Index Terms*
Refereed journal	

CHAPTER GOALS

The major focus of Chapter 2 is finding and critically reading research literature with an eye toward developing testable hypotheses. Your students should gain an understanding of the importance of conducting a literature review and how to go about doing one properly. You should introduce your students to using *PsycLit*, the *Psychological Abstracts,* and other indexes to locate relevant research. Don't assume that all of your students already know how to use the library and its resources. Key points for you to reinforce during class are

- How systematic and unsystematic observation can lead to the development of research ideas and testable hypotheses.
- How to develop good research questions (asking answerable questions, asking the right questions, and asking important questions).
- The relative advantages and disadvantages of using primary and secondary sources for a literature review.
- The relative advantages and disadvantages of using books, journal articles, and professional meetings as sources of research information.
- How to use PsycLit, the Psychological Abstracts, and other indexes to track down relevant literature.
- The advantages and disadvantages of using computers to do literature searches.
- How to read research articles critically.
- How to translate a general research question into a testable hypothesis.

IDEAS FOR CLASS ACTIVITIES

Using *PsycLit*

Having students actually conduct a search of *PsycLit* will reinforce the material in the text and provide a good refresher on how to conduct a literature search. Give students a broad, general topic (for example, memory, visual perception, or compliance) and have them first use the online version of the *Thesaurus of Psychological Index*

Terms to narrow the topic (for example, short-term memory, illusions, foot-in-the-door). Next, have students find five articles using *PsycLit* and write down all of the relevant bibliographic information.

Finally, have students find five research sources on a topic of their own choice. Instruct them to find articles relating to research that might be replicated in class. This is especially helpful if you are going to have students come up with their own project(s) for class.

Tracking Down Articles Based on Little Information

Provide students with minimal information about a source and have them find the full bibliographic citation using *PsycLit* or one of the other indexes (e.g., *Social Science Citations Index*). For example, give students the names of authors, date of publication, and the general topic and have them hunt down the full citation. The full citation should include all authors' names, the title of the article, full name of the journal, year, issue, and page numbers. Here are a few examples:

Weiner, B. (1993)—Sin versus Sickness
Greene, E., & Dodge, M. (1995)—Influence of a defendant's prior record
Byrnes, J. P., & Takahira, S. (1993)—Gender differences on the SAT

It is a good idea to use a lab period and be present for this exercise. We have found that students have many questions about using the *Citations Index*. For example, they are surprised to find the name of the journal in abbreviated form. They may need guidance on how to decipher the journal name and other information in the citation.

An extension of this exercise is to have students pick one of the topics previously used and find five more articles on that topic using *PsycLit* or the *Psychological Abstracts* (the five new citations must not be found in the reference section of the original article found in the *Citations Index*). Have students provide the following information:

1. The key words used in a *PsycLit* search, or the major heading and any subheadings in the *Psychological Abstracts* under which each reference was found.

2. If the *Psychological Abstracts* were used, have students provide the year and volume number of the *Psychological Abstracts* edition in which the reference was found.

3. The abstract number of each reference found.

4. The full reference for each article found (author names, title of the article, journal name, volume, issue, and page numbers).

Reading an Article

A useful exercise is to have students read and content-analyze a research article. This will get them used to reading primary sources and also show them how a research report should be written (which will be useful when they have to write their own lab reports or papers). You can either assign students to read specific articles you choose or have them find and analyze their own.

Have students do the following while they read the article:

1. Summarize the information contained in the abstract.

2. Write down the major purpose of the study.

3. Summarize the introduction. Have them pay specific attention to the topics presented, the reference citations provided, and how reference citations were used.

4. Evaluate why the author(s) chose to include the information found in the introduction.

5. List the hypotheses of the study.

6. Evaluate whether the hypotheses follow logically from the arguments presented in the introduction.

7. Briefly summarize the information contained in each of the subsections included under the method section.

8. Evaluate whether there is sufficient information in each section to allow the study to be replicated. If they think there is not, have them list what is missing.

9. If the article describes an experiment, list the variables manipulated by the researchers and the behaviors measured. If a correlational study is described, list the variables that were measured.

10. Evaluate the adequacy of the measures for testing the hypothesis.

11. Specify any control measures taken to rule out alternative explanations (for example, factors held constant, special subject samples).

12. List the major findings of the study as reported in the results.

13. Show how statistics were used to determine the significance of the findings (what statistics were reported and how they were used).

14. Summarize and evaluate the information in the discussion. Did the author's conclusions follow logically from the results reported (why or why not)? Did the author stray too far from the data when speculating on the meaning of the results? Were any alternative explanations offered for the results (if so, what were they)? What future research can be suggested?

15. Indicate whether the study adequately evaluated the hypotheses stated in the introduction. Why or why not?

Doing a Literature Search Online

Have your students do a literature search using the *CARL* database available on the Internet. Have each student choose a topic to research and generate a list of relevant references. Each student should evaluate the *CARL* system for ease of use, quality of information obtained, and availability of articles via fax. Finally, have students compare the bibliographic information obtained from *CARL* with the same information obtained with *PsycLit*. What differences exist?

Internet Resources for Using *PsycLit*

The American Psychological Association's Web site has a nice instructional document on using *PsycLit*. It can be found at the following address:

<http://www.apa.org/psychinfo/yellow.html#subject>

Before sending your students to the library to conduct a literature search, have them go to this Web site to learn about (or brush up on) the *PsycLit* skills. At this Web site students will find search aids, example journal, book, and chapter records, advanced searching techniques, and general search hints. There is also a quick reference guide to using *PsycLit*.

CHAPTER 3

CHOOSING A RESEARCH DESIGN

KEY QUESTIONS TO CONSIDER

- How are correlational and causal relationships similar and how are they different?
- What features of research allow you to draw causal inferences from your data?
- What are the defining features of correlational research?
- Why is it inappropriate to make causal inferences from correlational data?
- Under what conditions is correlational research preferred to experimental research?
- What is the relationship between the independent and dependent variables in an experiment?
- How do extraneous variables affect your research and what can you do to control them?
- What is the value of a demonstration and how does one differ from a true experiment?
- What is internal validity and why is it important?
- How do confounding variables threaten the internal validity of your research and how can they be avoided?
- What is external validity? Must all studies have strong external validity? Why or why not?
- What is a simulation and why would you use one?
- How does the realism of a simulation relate to the validity of the results obtained?
- What are the defining features of laboratory and field research?
- What are the relative advantages and disadvantages of doing laboratory and field research?

CHAPTER OUTLINE

Functions of a Research Design
Causal Versus Correlational Relationships
Correlational Research
    Characteristics of Correlational Research
    An Example of Correlational Research
        Assessing the Belsky and Rovine Study
    Causation and the Correlational Approach
        The Third-Variable Problem
        The Directionality Problem
    Why Use Correlational Research?
        Gathering Data in the Early Stages of Research
        Inability to Manipulate Variables
        Relating Naturally Occurring Variables
Experimental Research
    Characteristics of Experimental Research
        Manipulation of Independent Variables
        Control Over Extraneous Variables
    An Example of Experimental Research
        Assessing the Rauh et al. Experiment
    Strengths and Limitations of the Experimental Approach
    Experiments Versus Demonstrations
Internal and External Validity

KEY TERMS

Causal relationship	Experimental group
Correlational relationship	Control group
Correlational research	Extraneous variable
Third-variable problem	Demonstration
Directionality problem	Internal validity
Experimental research	Confounding
Independent variable	External validity
Treatment	Simulation
Dependent variable	

CHAPTER GOALS

The major theme to reinforce in Chapter 3 is the distinction between correlational and experimental research. You should first make a special effort to distinguish causal from correlational relationships. Students often have trouble separating the two. After reading Chapter 3, students should know how experimental and correlational research differ in execution and in the inferences that can be drawn from the data.

Students also learn in Chapter 3 the factors that affect internal and external validity, the relative advantages and disadvantages of field and laboratory research, what simulations are, and how simulations are used.

The following specific points should be discussed in class:

- The functions of a research design.
- The defining qualities of correlational and causal relationships between variables.
- The defining characteristics of correlational research.
- Why causal inferences should not logically be drawn from the results of a correlational study.
- The reasons why one might use correlational research.
- The defining characteristics of experimental research and how it differs from correlational research.
- The features of an experiment that allow you to draw causal inferences.
- The definition of extraneous variables and why they should be controlled.
- The strengths and weaknesses of the experimental approach.
- The distinction between a true experiment and a demonstration.
- The definition of internal validity.
- The threats to internal validity including confounding variables and extraneous variables.

- The definition of external validity, along with a discussion of Mook's idea that external validity is not absolutely necessary for all types of research.
- The threats to external validity.
- The relationship between internal and external validity.
- The defining characteristics and relative advantages of laboratory and field research.
- The defining characteristics of a simulation and how one is constructed.
- The issues of mundane and experimental realism of simulations.

IDEAS FOR CLASS ACTIVITIES

Demonstrations Versus Experiments

Chapter 3 distinguishes between demonstrations and experiments. The example cited in the text (subliminal messages) can be reinforced by presenting your class with another demonstration and analyzing it in class. The following is a brief summary of a demonstration that you can present (the full reference follows):

> Subjects, believing that they were going to complete a personality inventory, were seated in a chemistry classroom facing a large cabinet. There were three signs posted on the cabinet saying: "DANGER," "KEEP OUT," and "Attention: Cabinet Contains Hazardous Chemicals Intended ONLY for Animal Research. Possible Harm to Humans if Exposed!!! DO NOT OPEN." Inside the cabinet was a sealed brown box. After one minute an "authority figure" entered the room. The authority figure was dressed in a police uniform. The authority figure said to the subject: "I am late for a meeting with your dean. I want you to get in that cabinet and take the box to the president's office immediately." The results showed that 13 of 17 subjects obeyed the authority figure, despite the signs posted on the cabinet.

Ask your class the following questions:

1. What is it about the study that makes it a demonstration and not a true experiment?
   [There is no control group. Only one level of an "independent variable" was included.]
2. What can be concluded from the results reported?
3. How could the study be made into a true experiment?
   [Add a control group]
4. Have your students think of a few hypotheses centering on the issue of obedience to authority. Ask them how the demonstration could be expanded to include an independent variable.

Source

Sackhoff, J., & Weinstein, L. (1988). The effects of potential self-inflicted harm on obedience to an authority figure. *Bulletin of the Psychonomic Society, 26,* 347–348.

Correlational Versus Causal Relationships

A major point made in Chapter 3 is that correlational designs do not allow you to draw causal inferences from data. To further reinforce this point, you can have students find examples in the research literature of correlational and experimental research and analyze them. Each student should find one example of a correlational study and one experiment. Have each student analyze his or her articles by evaluating the following:

1. What were the hypotheses evaluated in the study? How were they stated?
2. What was the design of the study? If correlational, what variables were measured? If experimental, what were the independent and dependent variables?
3. How were the data analyzed?
4. What conclusions did the author draw from the data? For this question, have students be particularly vigilant for examples of causal inferences being drawn from correlational data.
5. For the correlational study, have students consider whether the study could be conducted as an experiment. If it can, what would the independent and dependent variables be? Would the experiment be ethical?

A Simple Correlational Study

In the Study Guide we suggested that students conduct a simple correlational study to familiarize themselves with correlational research. You can use that idea for a class project looking for a relationship between weather and mood. For a few days have students keep track of weather conditions (you can have the class decide what they want to measure, how to quantify it, and where to find the information). You could have them record things like precipitation, barometric pressure, and temperature, or simply have them rate the weather on a scale ranging from one to ten (1 = very bad weather, 10 = very good weather).

For each day, have students also complete the following measure:

Date _____   Time _____ a.m./p.m. (circle one)

Think back over the course of this day. Indicate on the scales below how you felt. Do this by placing an "X" in the appropriate space.

Happy	___	___	___	___	___	___	___	Sad
Active	___	___	___	___	___	___	___	Passive
Unfriendly	___	___	___	___	___	___	___	Friendly*
Helpful	___	___	___	___	___	___	___	Unhelpful
Lethargic	___	___	___	___	___	___	___	Vigorous*
Unsatisfied	___	___	___	___	___	___	___	Satisfied*
Trustful	___	___	___	___	___	___	___	Untrustful
Fed-up	___	___	___	___	___	___	___	Tolerant*
Excitable	___	___	___	___	___	___	___	Calm*
Warm	___	___	___	___	___	___	___	Cold
Bold	___	___	___	___	___	___	___	Hesitant
Uncooperative	___	___	___	___	___	___	___	Cooperative*
Slow	___	___	___	___	___	___	___	Fast*
Bad	___	___	___	___	___	___	___	Good*
Weak	___	___	___	___	___	___	___	Strong*
Cruel	___	___	___	___	___	___	___	Kind*
Relaxed	___	___	___	___	___	___	___	Tense
Busy	___	___	___	___	___	___	___	Lazy
Negative	___	___	___	___	___	___	___	Positive*

In general, how would you rate your mood today? Indicate your answer by circling the number on the scale below that best reflects your mood today.

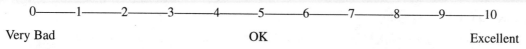

0———1———2———3———4———5———6———7———8———9———10

Very Bad   OK   Excellent

Data Analysis

Numerically code each of the bipolar adjectives by assigning the numbers 1–7 to the blanks. Rekey those adjective pairs that have the negative adjective first (the ones with the "*" above). Next obtain a sum for all of the adjective pairs. If you rekey the starred adjective pairs, then the LOWER the number the better the mood.

Have students record the data from the checklist and overall rating of mood, along with the weather data, on a data coding sheet. Next, perhaps using LabStat, have them run correlations between the weather data and mood.

Discuss with students what makes this study correlational. Have the students come up with interpretations for their findings, and discuss any methodological issues with them (for example, were the measures adequate?). Have students consider whether their results argue for a causal relationship between weather and mood. If no correlation was found, have students consider the reasons for failing to find a relationship (for example, inadequate measures).

If a correlation was found, have them think of alternative explanations for their results (for example, experimenter bias).

A Simple Experiment

Chapter 3 introduces students to the basics of experimental design. You can reinforce the text by having students conduct a simple, two-group experiment and analyze the results. Here is one example (which might serve as a nice follow-up to the obedience exercise previously presented):

Have students conduct an experiment on compliance. Have them pick a building entrance on campus that has several doors (perhaps the entrance to the psychology building, library, or student union). During a specified time period, have students simply count the number of people using each door. Prepare a sign saying "PLEASE USE OTHER DOOR" and post it on one of the doors at the same time the next day, and again have students count the number of people using each door.

To analyze the data, have students compare the number of people using the critical door with and without the sign. Students could assess the reliability of the results with a chi-square test.

You can use this simple experiment (or one of your own) to illustrate the following points:

1. The major characteristics of an experiment. The presence or absence of the sign constitutes the independent variable and the number of people using the critical door is the dependent variable.

2. The distinction between the experimental condition (sign present) and the control condition (sign absent), and how a relative comparison is made between the two.

3. If you use our suggested experiment, you will have the opportunity to discuss several aspects of research beyond the simple two-group design. Our sample experiment is a field experiment. You can discuss the differences between laboratory and field experimentation using this experiment as an example of the latter. Also, features of the suggested experiment relate to the issue of internal validity. For example, the experimental and control group are run on different days. This raises the possibility of an alternative explanation. Also, you can discuss the problem of exercising control over extraneous variables (e.g., the amount of traffic going through the door on different days or at different times) that might affect internal validity.

4. Finally, you can ask your class to develop a hypothesis about compliance and think about how an experiment like the suggested experiment could be carried out. What would the independent and dependent variables be? What steps would be taken to control extraneous and confounding variables?

Research Methods Tutorials on the Internet

A tutorial on various issues concerning research design can be found at the Cornell University Web site at the following address (which was valid at the time of this writing):

<http://trochim.human.cornell.edu/tutorial/TUTORIAL.HTM>

At this Web site your students can find information on choosing a research design that steps students through a series of yes/no question concerning design issues (for example, correlational or experimental design, pretest–posttest design or posttest only). The information contained in this document is relatively limited (that is, only a two-group randomized design is shown). Other menu items that students may find useful cover internal validity, categorical data analysis, correlational research designs, and ethical dilemmas.

As a class activity you could have your students visit this Web site and go through the "choosing a research design" tutorial to reinforce some of the points made in Chapter 3 about when correlational and experimental designs are used. They could also use the "correlational designs" tutorial to reinforce the material in the text on when these designs are used and their limitations.

CHAPTER 4

MAKING SYSTEMATIC OBSERVATIONS

KEY QUESTIONS TO CONSIDER

- What factors should you consider when deciding what to observe in a study?
- What is the reliability of a measure?
- How does the concept of reliability apply to different types of measures?
- What is meant by the accuracy of a measure?
- How do the reliability and accuracy of a measure affect the generality of a study?
- What is the validity of a measure?
- What are the ways you can assess the validity of a measure?
- What is the relationship between the validity and reliability of a measure?
- What information about a measure is conveyed by each of Steven's four "scales of measurement"? Do all measures fall neatly into one of those categories?
- What factors should be considered when choosing a scale of measurement?
- What is ecological validity and why should you be concerned about it?
- What is meant by the adequacy of a dependent measure?
- What two problems affect the adequacy of a dependent variable?
- Under what conditions would you consider tailoring your dependent measures to your research participants?
- What are the defining characteristics of the three types of dependent variables? What are the advantages and disadvantages of each?
- How can the act of measurement affect responses?
- What are role attitude cues, and how might they affect your study?
- What are demand characteristics and experimenter bias?
- What techniques can you use to reduce reactivity in research?
- What is a pilot study and why are they used?
- What are manipulation checks and why should you include them in your research?

CHAPTER OUTLINE

Deciding What to Observe
Choosing Specific Variables for Your Study
    Research Tradition
    Theory
    Availability of New Techniques
    Availability of Equipment
Choosing Your Measures
    Reliability of a Measure
        Reliability of a Physical Measure
        Reliability of Population Estimates
        Reliability of Judgments or Ratings by Multiple Observers
        Reliability of Psychological Tests or Measures
    Accuracy of a Measure

KEY TERMS

Reliability
Test–retest reliability
Parallel forms reliability
Split-half reliability
Accuracy
Validity
Face validity
Content validity
Criterion-related validity
Concurrent validity
Predictive validity
Construct validity
Nominal scale
Ordinal scale

Interval scale
Ratio scale
Range effects
Behavioral measure
Physiological measure
Self-report measure
Demand characteristics
Role attitude cues
Experimenter bias
Expectancy effects
Single-blind
Double-blind
Pilot study
Manipulation checks

CHAPTER GOALS

Chapter 4 introduces students to the general principles of systematic observation; specific techniques are discussed later in the text within the research design chapters (6–10). After reading this chapter, students should know how to select variables to include in a study, the characteristics of a measure (reliability, validity, accuracy, scale of measurement), how to evaluate the adequacy of a dependent measure, types of dependent measures, the problems created by reactivity, demand characteristics, and experimenter bias, and techniques to evaluate and deal with those problems. Your classroom lectures and discussions might focus on the following:

- Creating operational definitions for variables. Although operational definitions are explained in Chapter 2, students can always use more practice operationalizing variables, and should be reminded that an operational definition is a two-edged sword, making precise observation possible but at the expense of restricting the generality of findings.
- How research tradition, theory, and invention of new methods, techniques, instruments, and equipment influence the choice of specific variables to include in a study.
- How the reliability of a measure is defined and established, and how reliability relates to different types of measures (physical, population estimates, ratings by multiple observers, and psychological tests).
- What the accuracy of a measure refers to and why it is important to consider accuracy.
- How the validity of a measure is established and the kinds of validity different methods produce.
- The relationships between reliability, accuracy, and validity.
- What scales of measurement exist and how the scale of measurement determines the information that can be obtained from a measure and the statistics that can be legitimately applied to the data.
- What factors should be evaluated when choosing a scale of measurement.
- How the sensitivity of a dependent measure, range effects, and the nature of the subjects affect the usefulness of a dependent measure.
- What broad types of dependent variables exist (behavioral, physiological, and self-report measures).
- The reactive nature of psychological measurement, including the effects of demand characteristics, subject attitudes, and experimenter bias, and techniques to deal with these problems.
- What a pilot study is and why it is essential to conduct one before conducting one's main experiment.
- What are manipulation checks and why should you include them in your research?

IDEAS FOR CLASS ACTIVITIES

Psychological Ruler

This demonstration illustrates how psychological scales are constructed while providing insight into the problems of validity, reliability, and accuracy of a measure. Provide students with a simple response sheet similar to the one illustrated on the following page.

Psychological Ruler Study

Observer _____   Date _____

Participant   Height

_____
        | | |
        Very Short   Average   Very Tall

_____
        | | |
        Very Short   Average   Very Tall

_____
        | | |
        Very Short   Average   Very Tall

_____
        | | |
        Very Short   Average   Very Tall

_____
        | | |
        Very Short   Average   Very Tall

_____
        | | |
        Very Short   Average   Very Tall

_____
        | | |
        Very Short   Average   Very Tall

_____
        | | |
        Very Short   Average   Very Tall

_____
        | | |
        Very Short   Average   Very Tall

_____
        | | |
        Very Short   Average   Very Tall

There are enough spaces on each response sheet for ten observations. Each student should receive enough sheets to record one observation for each student in the class (for example, a class of 30 would require 3 sheets per student).

The spaces under the label "Participant" are for identifying labels (numbers work well), one for each student observed. You could have your class simply number the students consecutively as they are "measured."

Data Collection

Ask students to come, one at a time, to the front of the class. The rest of the students then rate the participant's height by marking the appropriate point along the scale for that observation. (Be sure each participant rates himself or herself at this time as well!)

When everyone in the class has been observed and rated, have the students actually measure each other's heights using a ruler (measuring to the nearest centimeter using a meter stick works well and avoids fractional measurements).

Data Analysis

Have students convert their ratings to numbers by measuring in millemeters from the bottom tick mark to the observation mark. Then have them collect all ratings for each subject and place them on a data coding sheet. They should create one column for each subject. Have them then average the scores in each column. Below this average, have them place the subject's actual height as measured.

At this point, your students will have two scores for each subject: the rated height and the measured height. Have your students plot the rated height (y-axis) against the measured height (x-axis). What usually emerges is a reasonable approximation of a straight line, with some degree of scatter about it. Have the students eyeball a best-fitting straight line to the data points.

There are a number of things you can do at this point. You can show students how they could use the relationship they have uncovered to estimate actual height from the average ratings. This provides a nice springboard for discussing such issues as the reliability or repeatability of the measurements and how averaging over repeated observations can increase the reliability. It is also a nice example where the external validity of a measure is established by comparison with an accepted measure (concurrent validity). You might point out that if rating scales can provide valid measures of objective quantities such as height, we should have some confidence that they can provide valid measures of psychological states for which objective physical measures are lacking.

Research Examples

Perhaps the best way students learn how variables are chosen, operationalized, and measured is by going over specific examples in the literature. Bring in a number of primary research articles and have students identify the variables employed in each study. Have them provide both a general name for each variable (e.g., "anxiety") and the specific operational definition used by the study (e.g., manifest anxiety scale). Note the potential difficulty of generalizing the results to the more general concept, and the possibility that different operational definitions might lead to different conclusions.

You might then ask your students to identify the type of dependent measure(s) employed and the scale of measurement, and discuss with them how the scale of measurement relates to the statistics the authors of the study used in their analysis of the data.

Role Playing

To bring home the reactive nature of psychological measurement, including the influences of demand characteristics, participant attitudes, and experimenter bias, you can have your students play the roles of participant and experimenter in a blatantly biased "experiment." This is particularly effective if students are given the chance to play the participant in both the experimental and control groups so that they can contrast their treatments by the experimenter. In the experimental condition, the experimenter would practically help the participant to make the correct responses (giving hints, clearly explaining what to do, etc.). In the control condition, the experimenter would be almost obstructive (e.g., refusing to explain unclear instructions, being seemingly uninterested in the participant, etc.). After the demonstration, ask students what could be done to minimize these problems.

CHAPTER 5

CHOOSING AND USING SUBJECTS

KEY QUESTIONS TO CONSIDER

- What factors affect your decision to use animal subjects or human participants?
- What is a population and how does it relate to a sample?
- What is a sample and how is it used in research?
- What is random sampling and how does it affect the generality of your research?
- What is nonrandom sampling and how does it relate to the generality of your research?
- Under what conditions is random sampling preferred over nonrandom sampling?
- Why did the APA code of research ethics evolve?
- What are the historical roots of the APA code of research ethics?
- What are the main points contained in the APA code of research ethics?
- What role does the institutional review board play in research?
- How can ethical guidelines affect how you conduct and interpret your research?
- How does the nature of your research affect how you will acquire human participants?
- How does the requirement of voluntary participation affect the validity of your research?
- How do participant characteristics and situational factors relate to one's decision to volunteer for research?
- How can volunteerism affect the internal and external validity of your research?
- What can you do to reduce the problem of volunteerism in research?
- What is deception in research and when is it allowed?
- What effect does deception have on your participants?
- What are the solutions to the problem of deception? What are the advantages and disadvantages of each solution?
- Why would you consider using animals as subjects in your research?
- What affects your decision about which animal to use in research and how can the chosen animal be obtained?
- What ethical guidelines must you follow when using animals as subjects in research?
- Must the results from animal research generalize to humans? Why or why not?
- What arguments have animal rights activists made against using animals in research? How have scientists addressed the issues raised by animal rights activists?
- What alternatives to using animals in research have been proposed? What are the advantages and disadvantages of those techniques?

CHAPTER OUTLINE

Using Subjects: General Considerations
    Populations and Samples
    Sampling and Generalization
    Is Random Sampling Always Necessary?
Considerations When Using Human Participants
    Ethical Research Practice
        Nazi War Crimes and the Nuremberg Code
        APA Ethical Guidelines
        Government Regulations

KEY TERMS

Population	Volunteer bias
Sample	Deception
Generalization	Role playing
Random sample	Debriefing
Nonrandom sample	Institutional animal care and use committee (IACUC)
Institutional review board (IRB)	

CHAPTER GOALS

Three major themes are developed in Chapter 5: the issue of sampling from a population and the generality of research results, ethical treatment of human participants and animal subjects, and the interface between the requirements of ethical research practice and the validity of research results. It is important for you to stress the idea that the goal of research is to make general statements about a population based on a small sample drawn from that population. You should emphasize how using convenient samples (e.g., college students) and ethical research practices affect the validity of research results. Some key points to hit during class are

- The definitions of population, sample, and generalization.
- The difference between random and nonrandom sampling and when random sampling is necessary and when it is not.
- How the nature of the research sample affects generalization.

- The history of the emergence of the APA ethical code.
- The ten major points of the Nuremberg Code, the APA code of ethics, and the main points of the HHS guidelines.
- The factors that affect a potential participant's decision to participate in research.
- How the requirements of voluntary participation and informed consent affect the internal and external validity of research results.
- The remedies that have been proposed for the problem of volunteerism.
- The ethical versus methodological issues surrounding using deception in research and what steps can be taken to avoid the negative side effects of deception.
- How debriefing should be used, especially in research using deception.
- The contributions of research using animals as subjects and the generality of the results of animal research.
- The major points of the APA ethical code for using animals in research.
- The issues of whether research with animals should be done and the generality of animal research data.
- The issues surrounding the animal rights movement and how scientists address the concerns of animal rights activists.
- The alternatives to using live animals in research and the efficacy of those alternatives.

IDEAS FOR CLASS ACTIVITIES

Ethical Dilemmas

One of the major themes developed in Chapter 5 is the importance of considering the impact of research on its subjects. Following are several research examples (some of which are included in the study guide) illustrating a wide range of research methods and subjects. Have students evaluate each of the examples for the following questions:

1. Overall, are there any ethical issues that should be raised concerning the research described?

2. What specific ethical problems can be identified in each example (e.g., invasion of privacy, deception, stress, debriefing, and so on)?

3. How could the ethical problems be remedied? That is, what steps could a researcher take to ensure that subjects are treated ethically? (For this question, tell students not to worry about how the validity of the study would be affected.)

4. How would any remedies for ethical issues impact on the internal and external validity of the results of each research example?

After each of the dilemmas, we have included a brief synopsis of the ethical issues raised. Keep in mind that these are not necessarily ethical *problems*. Rather, they are issues that should be raised to help students gain a greater sensitivity to ethical issues.

1. Middlemist, Knowles, and Matter (1976) conducted a study investigating whether or not invasions of personal space are physiologically as well as psychologically arousing. The experiment was run in a men's lavatory, in which the investigators closed off one or another urinal. Participants were forced to urinate either in the urinal next to a male confederate of the experimenter or in the urinal one away from the confederate. A second confederate positioned in a toilet stall adjacent to the urinals observed the subjects via periscope and recorded the latency to onset of urination and its duration.

[There are several ethical issues to discuss with your class in this research example. First, the issue of invasion of privacy comes up. Should researchers be observing a behavior that our culture deems as private, even though that behavior is occurring in a semiprivate place (a public lavatory)? Second, the issue of informed consent should be raised. Participants did not give prior consent to be in the study. Ask your students how obtaining true informed consent would affect the validity of the results (prior consent would lead to a biased sample because only those participants who agree to be in the experiment could be included and once participants know about the experiment their behavior may be affected). Have students think about how the problem of informed consent could be circumvented. One possibility is to obtain consent after the participants have been observed (perhaps by another experimenter outside the lavatory). Discuss the problems this could raise (biased sample). Finally, should the participants be debriefed? What consequences might this have for participants? Have students think about an effective debriefing procedure for this experiment.]

2. In a classic experiment on cognitive dissonance theory, Festinger and Carlsmith (1959) had participants engage in an extremely boring task. After doing this task, participants were asked if they would help out in the experiment with the next participant because the regular assistant did not show up. The accomplice-participants were asked to tell the next participant that the task was really interesting and exciting. For telling this little white lie the accomplice-participant was told that he would be paid (either $1 or $20, depending on the condition to which he was assigned). The experiment was actually designed to see if the amount of money promised affected the accomplice-participant's attitude toward the boring task. At the end of the experiment, participants were asked to return the money.

[Students normally focus on the fact that participants were asked to give back the money they had been paid. You could discuss the ethics of promising participants something and then reneging on that promise. Because participants were *asked* to return the money, there is probably no ethical violation. A second issue is the fact that participants were induced to lie. This may lead to subtle shifts in the participants' self-perceptions (they may have come into the experiment believing they were honest and left with some doubts). Is it ethical to induce participants to perform a behavior our culture discourages? Have students discuss this issue. Also, discuss the issue of informed consent. How could it be obtained without reducing the validity of the results? Finally, have students design an effective debriefing session to reduce any negative effects of the experiment.]

3. In his classic study of obedience to authority, Milgram (1963) led participants to believe they were administering painful shocks to another participant (actually a confederate of the experimenter who was receiving no shocks) in a bogus learning experiment. Participants were told that each time the "learner" made a mistake, an electric shock of increasing intensity (15–450 volts) must be delivered. In some conditions the "learner" screamed and pounded on the wall. If the participant expressed reluctance to continue, the experimenter told him that he "must go on." The experiment actually examined whether participants would obey the experimenter's orders to continue delivering shocks.

[As you probably know, Milgram was criticized for the ethics of this famous study. Several ethical issues are raised in this example. First, participants were successfully deceived into believing they were administering shocks. This would be a good opportunity to discuss the possibility of using role-playing as an alternative to the method used by Milgram. Have students consider whether the results obtained in a role-playing study would parallel Milgram's (they most likely would not). Second, discuss the issue of informed consent. How could informed consent be obtained for this experiment while preserving the power of the situation? (Discuss the possibility of informing participants that the experiment would involve high levels of stress, without specifying the source. If this were done, raise the possibility of ending up with a biased sample because only those participants who think they could endure the stress would remain in the experiment. Would including the caveat of "withdrawing at any time" in an informed consent form affect the results?) Third, discuss the shifts that might occur in participants' self-perception. Finally, discuss the importance of following up with debriefing. Discuss the need for long-term follow-up (which Milgram included) in an experiment such as this.]

4. In a simulation study of plea bargaining, Gregory, Mowen, and Linder (1978) gave false feedback to undergraduate participants. Participants waited in a waiting room for an experiment to begin. In one condition, another participant who had just been in the experiment (actually a confederate of the experimenter) told the waiting participant that most of the answers to the test that would be taken are "B." In a second condition no information was given to the waiting participant. After the participant took the test, the experimenter accused the participant of cheating and told him that it was a serious matter that would have to be presented to a review board for action. Participants were led to believe that the consequences of the accused cheating were severe. The participants were told that if they admitted cheating they would simply lose credit for participating in the experiment.

[The main point in this example is that participants were placed in a highly stressful situation in which they were deceived. Discussions could parallel those centering on the Milgram experiment. Issues of adequate informed consent, stress, debriefing, and so on should be discussed.]

5. In a field experiment conducted by Harari, Harari, and White (1985), male participants walking alone or in groups were exposed to a simulated rape. As participants walked along a path to a parking lot, a male and female confederate of the experimenters acted out a simulated rape (The male grabbed the female around the waist, put his hand over her mouth, and dragged her into some bushes. The female screamed for help.). Observers stationed at various points recorded the number of participants who offered help. Prior to actual intervention, participants were stopped and told of the true purpose of the experiment. The results showed that 85% of the participants walking in groups offered help to the victim, whereas 65% of the participants walking alone offered help. Support was found for the idea that individuals in groups are as likely, if not more likely, to help when the victim is clearly in need of help.

[Because this is a field experiment, prior informed consent was not obtained from participants. Have the class discuss whether informed consent could have been obtained. You might point out that informed consent might be waived by an IRB if the researchers can demonstrate the potential importance of the research results. You can discuss the possibility of obtaining post hoc informed consent (participants are to be asked for consent *after* they participate in the experiment). Other issues to raise are the ethics of exposing participants to a highly stressful event and the unpredictability of the participants' reactions to it (for example, what if one participant had a gun and used it?). Harari et al. make no mention of debriefing. Should participants be stopped and debriefed after the experiment? How about those participants who chose not to help? How should they be debriefed? You can use this example to start a discussion of the ethical issues surrounding field experimentation.]

6. In order to test the effects of controllability on stress responses, Weiss (1971) administered electric shock to rats. Three rats were run together in a yolked procedure. One rat in the triad could avoid or escape the electric shock by making a response. A second rat received the same number of shocks of the same duration as the first rat but could neither avoid nor escape them. The third rat received no shocks. Immediately after the experimental session the rats were removed from the test chambers and sacrificed. Their stomachs were then inspected for ulcers. The rats that lacked control over the shock had developed extensive lesioning, whereas neither the control rats (those receiving no shocks) nor those that could avoid or escape the shock showed much damage.

[Some students may react to the use of electric shock in this (and other) studies. Use this example to reinforce the points about ethical treatment of animals in research. Discuss the cost–benefit ratio: Are the results of this study (and similar studies) important enough to warrant using electric shock? Who should make such a decision? Another aspect of your discussion could focus on the sacrificing of the animals to inspect their stomachs. Was there a need to sacrifice the animals (are there alternatives)? Were the rats sacrificed humanely? You can use this example to discuss whether the alternatives to using animals in research discussed in the text could be used in behavioral research.]

References for Ethical Dilemmas

Festinger, L., & Carlsmith, J. M. (1959). Cognitive consequences of forced compliance. *Journal of Abnormal and Social Psychology, 58,* 203–210.

Gregory, W. L., Mowen, J. C., & Linder, D. E. (1978). Social psychology and plea bargaining: Applications, methodology and theory. *Journal of Personality and Social Psychology, 36,* 1521–1530.

Harari, H., Harari, O., & White, R. V. (1985). The reaction to rape by American male bystanders. *Journal of Social Psychology, 125,* 653–658.

Middlemist, R. D., Knowles, E. S., & Matter, C. F. (1976). Personal space invasions in the lavatory: Suggestive evidence for arousal. *Journal of Personality and Social Psychology, 33,* 541–546.

Milgram, S. (1963). Behavioral study of obedience. *Journal of Abnormal Psychology, 67,* 371–378.

Weiss, J. M. (1971). Effects of coping behavior in different warning signal conditions on stress pathology in rats. *Journal of Comparative and Physiological Psychology, 77,* 1–13.

Simulating an IRB

In Chapter 5 the institutional review board was discussed. For this exercise assign students to research groups (which you could do early in the semester in preparation for this exercise). Have each research group come up with a research idea and develop a proposal for their study, specifying the subjects to be used, materials, procedures, informed consent, and strategies to protect participants. Once students have developed their proposals, have each research group assume the role of an institutional review board and evaluate the other groups' research proposals. Have them screen each proposal according to the APA ethical guidelines outlined in Chapter 5. If any ethical problems are encountered, the IRBs should identify them and recommend remedies.

After the proposals have been screened, you can lead a general class discussion of what ethical problems arose and how they might be eliminated. You should also discuss how the steps taken to remedy any ethical problems affect the validity of the results of each study.

Deception and Debriefing

Have students go to the library and find an article or two that used deception (the best bet is to look in social psychological journals like *The Journal of Personality and Social Psychology, The Journal of Experimental Social Psychology, The Journal of Applied Social Psychology, The Journal of Social Psychology,* or *Basic and Applied Social Psychology*). Have students make a photocopy of each article they find and evaluate it for the following:

1. What form of deception was used (active or passive)?

2. Specifically, what did the deception involve?

3. Were the participants debriefed? Is so, what did that debriefing involve?

4. Have students think about how they would feel if they had been deceived as the actual participants were deceived. Would debriefing make a difference in how they might feel?

As an extension to this exercise, have each student present his or her findings to the class and then lead the class in a discussion of the need for the deception, possible alternatives to deception, and how to effectively debrief participants.

CHAPTER 6

USING NONEXPERIMENTAL DESIGNS

KEY QUESTIONS TO CONSIDER

- What are the defining characteristics of observational research?
- How do observational techniques apply to both nonexperimental and experimental research?
- How are behavioral categories used in observational research developed?
- What are the major techniques used to make behavioral observations in observational research?
- What is the distinction between recording single events and behavior sequences?
- What are the sampling techniques used to handle complexity in observational research?
- Why and how would you evaluate interrater reliability?
- How do you deal with data from multiple observers?
- What are the sources of bias in observational research and what techniques can be used to reduce it?
- What is the difference between quantitative and qualitative data? What are the problems inherent in collecting qualitative data?
- What are naturalistic observation and unobtrusive observation? How are they used to study behavior?
- What are some of the advantages and disadvantages of naturalistic observation?
- What is ethnography and what are some of the important issues facing a field ethnographer?
- How are data recorded and analyzed in ethnography?
- What are the defining characteristics of sociometry? In what capacities can sociometry be used?
- How are the case history method and archival research used?
- What is content analysis and what steps are taken when using it?

CHAPTER OUTLINE

Conducting Observational Research
    Developing Behavioral Categories
    Quantifying Behavior in an Observational Study
        Frequency Method
        Duration Method
        Intervals Method
    Recording Single Events or Behavior Sequences
    Coping With Complexity
        Time Sampling
        Individual Sampling
        Event Sampling
        Recording
    Establishing the Reliability of Your Observations
        Percent Agreement
        Cohen's Kappa
        Pearson's Product–Moment Correlation
        Dealing With Data From Multiple Observers
    Sources of Bias in Observational Research
Qualitative Approaches

KEY TERMS

Behavioral categories	Nonparticipant observation
Interrater reliability	Sociometry
Qualitative data	Sociogram
Naturalistic observation	Case history
Ethnography	Archival research
Participant observation	Content analysis

CHAPTER GOALS

Chapter 6 introduces several examples of nonexperimental research. The opening section of the chapter discusses issues related to observational research: developing behavioral categories, quantifying behavior, and assessing interrater reliability. Students should learn that observational research is as involved as any other form of research. Next, students are introduced to various nonexperimental techniques (e.g., naturalistic observation, ethnography, participant and nonparticipant observation, sociometry, content analysis). The pros and cons of each technique should be reinforced. In class you can focus on the following:

- How behavioral categories are developed and the importance of clear category definitions.
- How researchers cope with the complexities inherent in observational research by adopting different observation techniques.
- The distinction between recording single events and behavior sequences, and why you might want to record behavior sequences.
- How different sampling techniques (e.g., time sampling, individual sampling) are used to cope with complexity in observational research.
- How percent agreement, Cohen's Kappa, and the Pearson correlation can be used to establish interrater reliability.
- How data from multiple observers are handled.

- The sources of bias in observational research and the techniques that are used to reduce bias.
- The distinction between quantitative and qualitative data, and some of the special problems posed by collecting qualitative data.
- The defining qualities of naturalistic observation and techniques for making unobtrusive observations, along with the advantages and disadvantages of this technique.
- The defining characteristics of ethnography and the issues facing an ethnographer (e.g., participant versus nonparticipant observation, obtaining access to a field setting, gaining entry into a group).
- How observations are made, data recorded and analyzed in ethnography.
- The defining characteristics of sociometry and how it can be used in observational research.
- The defining characteristics of the case history method and archival research.
- How a content analysis is done, including the distinction between recording and context units, and the requirements for doing high-quality content analyses.

IDEAS FOR CLASS ACTIVITIES

Observational Research I

To introduce your students to observational research, have them conduct a small-scale observational study. Note that this exercise might take two or three class periods because students will be designing their own measures, defining behaviors, and carrying out behavioral observations. It is a good idea to plan for this exercise in your schedule.

Break your class up into small research groups (three or four per group works well) and have each group choose behavior to observe (they may choose from the ideas in the student study guide). Each group should come up with an operational definition of the behavior to be observed (for example, aggression is any act in which one child hits another), relevant behavioral categories, a coding sheet (patterned after the one shown in Chapter 6), an observation method, and a strategy for dealing with multiple observers and interrater reliability.

It is a good idea for you to sit in with each group to give them direction and help them develop their measures. However, let them come up with the idea and decide how to develop it, even if there are some flaws in their strategy. Often, students learn more about research by making some mistakes. Later you can discuss with the class what problems occurred within each group and how those problems could be rectified.

After each group has chosen a behavior and developed their observation scheme, have them actually make some behavioral observations. Once the data have been collected, have each group summarize its data and evaluate interrater reliability using one of the methods discussed in Chapter 6.

After all the groups have collected and summarized their data, have each group present its study to the class as a whole. Use this as an opportunity to point out important methodological issues to the class (e.g., operational definitions, how behavioral categories were defined, how behavior was observed, and any problems that were encountered). If problems were encountered, have the class analyze how those problems could have been avoided or how they might be handled in a second observational study.

Observational Research II

If you do not want to dedicate two or three class periods to carry out the first exercise, you can still conduct an observational study by assigning the class as a whole to do a single study (perhaps one of the ideas in the student study guide could be used). If you have a local zoo nearby, you can assign students to make observations of animal behavior. Perhaps subgroups of the class could observe different animals. The following observational study of primate behavior was suggested to us by our colleague Carol Lawton and is based on a project developed at the National Zoo in Washington, D.C. [Office of Education, National Zoological Park (1989). *A curriculum for high school students*. Washington, D.C., Smithsonian Institution]. This project gives students a good introduction to methods used in observational research.

Students go to the local zoo and, working in pairs, make behavioral observations of monkeys.

Materials

A data coding sheet with columns representing the behavioral categories to be observed and rows representing time intervals is needed for this project (a data coding sheet for this project is provided in Appendix I). Students should choose four behavioral categories and label the columns on the data coding sheet accordingly. Some suggestions for behavioral categories are eating, grooming, climbing, playing, and attending to the observers. Students should also rate the activity level shown by the animals within each time interval. A column for this, subdivided into four smaller columns (labeled 1, 2, 3, and 4, respectively), is provided on the coding sheet. Use the following scale to rate activity level:

1 = little movement
2 = movement of limbs, head, or trunk with the animal remaining in one position
3 = slow-paced locomotion from one location to another
4 = fast-paced locomotion

To signal observation periods, have students use portable tape recorders equipped with tapes that emit a beep every thirty seconds.

Procedure

Students should spend about 10 minutes making casual observations of the monkeys. From these observations the students should develop their four behavioral categories. Have students develop clear definitions for those behaviors. The four behaviors to be observed will be entered on the data sheet under the heading "BEHAVIORS."

For each 30-second interval, each student will place a check mark in the appropriate column for each behavior that occurs within the interval. Activity ratings should be made at the beep by checking one of the four levels.

For this project students will work in pairs, each making an independent set of observations of the same monkey at the same time. Give students an initial 5-minute practice session to familiarize themselves with the task and to work out any discrepancies or clarify definitions. The main observation period should last for at least 15 minutes. Students can repeat their observations for a second subject and then compare observations across subjects (optional).

Results

Once all observations have been made, students should conduct the following data analyses:

1. Choose data from a subject (if more than one was observed) and compute interrater reliabilities using Cohen's Kappa. A Cohen's Kappa should be computed for each of the four behavioral categories and for the activity level measure. In a lab report, students could discuss any disagreements between observers. How could disagreement be reduced?

2. Have students compute frequencies with which each behavior occurred and an average activity level. Have them evaluate which behaviors were most frequent and any differences observed across subjects.

3. Have students think back upon their observation period and record any difficulties that were encountered (e.g., complexity of the behaviors observed, difficulty making observations). Discuss with the class how these problems could be circumvented.

Content Analysis

A content analysis is a relatively easy and interesting research project for students to work on. Break your class into several research groups (again, three or four per group works well) and have them decide on something to content-analyze (television shows, magazine advertisements). Use the following set of guidelines for this project:

1. Choose something to content-analyze. Some possible areas are as follows:

    a. Sexism in children's literature.
    b. Aggression and violence in children's television programming.
    c. Images of men and women in magazine or television advertisements.
    d. Sexual or violent themes presented in music videos.

e. Racial portrayals in prime-time television.

f. Gender differences in the content of personal advertisements.

g. The content of "one-minute" speeches made by Republicans and Democrats on the floor of the U.S. Congress (access to CSPAN on cable television is needed).

2. Develop a research hypothesis that will be the focus of the content analysis. For example, if a group chooses to content-analyze music videos, you might develop a hypothesis about the frequency of sexual content in videos by male and female artists or in videos shown on MTV and VH-1. If sexism in children's literature is chosen, the hypothesis might focus on classics (e.g., "Cinderella") versus modern stories.

3. Generate a list of appropriate behavioral categories, recording units, and context units for your content analysis. A quick literature review might help students develop their categories and the recording units. A coding sheet should be devised that includes the recording and context units to be used.

4. Conduct the content analysis. This will involve finding and analyzing representative samples of the material. Students must give some thought as to how they will select materials to content-analyze.

5. Analyze and interpret the data. Data analysis should focus on

a. The frequencies within each behavioral category.

b. The differences across "groups" relevant to the hypothesis (e.g., did videos from MTV differ from those on VH-1? If so, how?).

c. Measures of interrater reliability.

d. Difficulties encountered when doing the content analysis (e.g., clearly defining recording units, finding materials, and so on).

6. Each research group should prepare a brief (10–15 minutes) talk to present to the class. The presentations allow class members to share their experiences and learn what the other groups did for their content analyses. The talk should include the following:

a. An outline of the topic under study.

b. A description of how the recording/context units were developed.

c. The method used to acquire materials for content analysis.

d. A description of how the content analysis was done.

e. A summary of the findings.

f. A discussion of any difficulties encountered when doing the analysis.

g. A discussion of the generality of the results. (Are there any methodological considerations that limit the conclusions you may draw from the results?)

Ethnography I: Participant Observation

In ethnography a qualitative, written record is made of observed behaviors. Have your students design and carry out an ethnographic study. They might, for example, study a group to which they belong (e.g., a bowling league, a church organization, a club) as a participant observer. Students should record the nature of the interactions that take place within the group, the hierarchical structure, if any, and perhaps even nonverbal cues (facial expressions, body language, and so on.). They should make careful notes of the behaviors they observe. Students should devise a method for observing behavior, making field notes, transcribing field notes, and analyzing their data.

Ethnography II: Nonparticipant Observation

Have students design and carry out a nonparticipant observation ethnographic study. Students should find a relatively crowded place (a shopping mall, skating rink, bowling alley, sporting event, an airport) and make careful observations of the people in that place. Both verbal (what people say to each other) and nonverbal (what people are doing) behaviors should be recorded. Students should work out a strategy for taking field notes and later making more complete notes at the end of the day. Students should also work out a strategy for remaining unobtrusive and for analyzing their data.

Sociometry (Berg, 1998)

Have students carry out a sociometric study of a group. The group could be a class, a club, or a sports team. Students should list the names of all members of the group on a piece of paper. Then, using the coding categories that follow, a number is placed next to each person's name indicating how they feel about that particular person. Note: The number one must be used only once and they should put the number zero by their own name. Each person in the group should complete the sociometric measure.

When all members of the group have completed the sociometric instrument, the results are to be summarized on a coding sheet similar to the one shown in Figure 6-5 and then shown graphically on a sociogram.

Sociometric Rating Instrument (Berg, 1998, reprinted with permission)

(Question/Choices)

Directions: On a separate sheet, write the name of everyone in your group or organization. Read the following paragraphs and place their corresponding numbers in front of every name for which they apply. You may use the number <u>one</u> only once, and please place only a single number by each name. By your own name, please place a zero.

My Very Best Friend

1. I would like to have this person as one of my very best friends. I would like to spend a great deal of time with this person. I think I could tell some of my problems and concerns to this person, and I would do everything I could to help this person with his or her problems and concerns. I will give a number 1 to my very best friend.

My Other Friend(s)

2. I would enjoy working and doing things with this person. I would invite this person to a party in my home, and I would enjoy going places with this person and our other friends. I would like to talk and do a variety of things with this person and to be with this person often. I want this person to be one of my friends. I will give a number 2 to every person who is my friend.

I Do Not Know This Person

3. I do not know this person very well. Maybe I would like this person if I got to know him or her; maybe I would not. I do not know whether I would like to spend time or work with this person. I will place a number 3 in front of the name of every person I do not know very well.

I Do Not Care for This Person

4. I will greet this person when I see him or her around school or in a store, but I do not enjoy being around this person. I might spend some time with this person—if I had nothing to do, or if I had a social obligation to attend where this person also was in attendance. I do not care for this person very much. I will place a number 4 in front of the name of every person I do not care for very much.

I Dislike This Person

5. I speak to this person only when it is necessary. I do not like to work or spend time with this person. I avoid serving on the same groups or committees with this person. I will place a number 5 in front of the name of every person I do not like.

CHAPTER 7

USING SURVEY RESEARCH

KEY QUESTIONS TO CONSIDER

- What are some of the applications of survey research?
- What are the steps involved in designing a questionnaire?
- How do open-ended and restricted questionnaire items differ? What are the advantages and disadvantages of each?
- How do you design effective rating scales?
- What general "rules" (precision, biased questions, and so on) should you follow when writing questionnaire items? What could happen if these "rules" are violated?
- How do you arrange your items on a questionnaire?
- What are the different methods of administering a questionnaire? What are the advantages and disadvantages of each?
- What techniques are used to assess the reliability of a questionnaire?
- How can the reliability of a questionnaire be increased?
- What techniques are used to assess the validity of a questionnaire?
- What is a biased sample and why should you work hard to avoid it?
- What are the characteristics of the various sampling techniques used in survey research?
- How do you determine the size of the sample needed for a valid survey?

CHAPTER OUTLINE

Survey Research
Designing Your Questionnaire
 Selecting the Questionnaire Format
  Types of Questionnaire Items
  Rating Scales
  Writing Questionnaire Items
 Assembling the Questionnaire
Administering Your Questionnaire
 Mail Surveys
  Combatting Nonresponse Bias
 Telephone Surveys
 Group Administration
 The Interview
 The Internet
Assessing the Reliability of a Questionnaire
 Assessing Reliability by Repeated Testing
 Assessing Reliability With a Single Test
 Increasing Reliability
Assessing the Validity of a Questionnaire
Acquiring a Sample for Your Survey
 Representativeness

KEY TERMS

Open-ended item	Representative sample
Restricted item	Biased sample
Partially open-ended item	Simple random sampling
Mail survey	Stratified sampling
Nonresponse bias	Proportionate sampling
Telephone survey	Systematic sampling
Interview	Cluster sampling
Test–retest reliability	Multistage sampling
Parallel-forms reliability	Sampling error
Split-half reliability	

CHAPTER GOALS

Chapter 7 introduces the specific techniques and general logic of survey methodology, beginning with questionnaire construction, then covering ways to administer the questionnaire (mail, telephone, group, face-to-face), assessing reliability and validity, and ending with sampling, including logic, issues, and specific sampling techniques. Your classroom discussions might focus on the following:

- The steps involved in designing a questionnaire.
- What demographics are, and the distinction between predictor and criterion variables.
- The types of questionnaire items and the advantages of each.
- How to design rating scales.
- How to write clear questionnaire items that minimize bias.
- How to organize the questionnaire to keep respondents interested in and clear about what they should be doing.
- The types of surveys, their relative advantages and disadvantages, and how they should be conducted.
- Techniques for assessing reliability and validity of a questionnaire.
- Sample representativeness.
- Types of sampling techniques and how to use each.
- How to determine an appropriate sample size.

IDEAS FOR CLASS ACTIVITIES

Attitude Questionnaire

The following is a laboratory exercise involving the construction and administration of an attitude questionnaire, and the analysis of the resulting data. For simplicity, you might want to use a convenience sample for this exercise (e.g., students in the university cafeteria or library) while reminding students that a professional survey would use some form of random sampling procedure and that, because we used a convenience sample, the population to which their results apply is not really known.

Attitude Questionnaire

I. Purpose and Overview

The purpose of this lab exercise is to introduce you to constructing a measurement instrument. For this exercise you will construct and evaluate an attitude questionnaire. After administering your questionnaire you will evaluate it for its reliability and for the internal consistency of items.

Each lab group will decide on a topic about which attitudes will be tested. Topics might include issues relating to current events (e.g., attitudes toward recycling, the president's policies), individual attitudes (sex-roles), or any other topic that interests you. The only restriction is that you choose a nonsensitive topic (e.g., don't develop a questionnaire on sexual or religious attitudes).

II. Format of the Questionnaire

Likert Items

Your questionnaire will consist of at least 15 Likert items measuring the same attitude. Likert items consist of a statement followed by a five-point rating scale on which the subject indicates the degree of agreement with the statement. For example:

	Strongly Disagree	Disagree	Neutral	Agree	Strongly Agree
The president is doing a good job cutting the federal budget.	1	2	3	4	5

Negatively and Positively Keyed Items

In order to reduce the chances of a response set bias, you should have some of your items positively keyed and some negatively keyed. A positively keyed item is one where agreement means a positive attitude toward the issue being evaluated. For example, the preceding item is positively keyed because a high score (strongly agree) means that the subject is generally favorable toward how the president is handling the budget deficit.

In contrast, a negatively keyed item is one where disagreement indicates a positive attitude. For example:

	Strongly Disagree	Disagree	Neutral	Agree	Strongly Agree
The president is not doing a good job cutting the federal budget.	1	2	3	4	5

Disagreement with this item indicates a generally favorable attitude toward how the president is handling budget cutting. Try, if you can, to have half of your items positively keyed and half negatively keyed.

Demographic/Predictor Items

In addition to the Likert items evaluating subjects' attitudes, you should come up with a few items (four or five perhaps) that evaluate something about the subjects. These items should be ones that you feel will correlate with the attitude measured on your questionnaire. Some examples, relevant to the above example, might be:

Political party affiliation (Republican/Democrat)

Educational level

Occupation

Income

Whatever you choose to measure, keep in mind that these items must also be carefully constructed (see Chapter 7 in the text for information on how to construct questionnaire items). Design these with an eye toward correlating them with attitudes.

In addition to the questionnaire items, you will have to develop a set of instructions that generally explain how the questionnaire is set up and how to complete the specific types of items included on the questionnaire.

Also, you will have to develop an appropriate informed consent form (see Chapter 5 in the text for an example of an informed consent form). The informed consent form must contain the following:

1. A statement that the survey is being conducted as a requirement for your Research Methods class.

2. A statement about the topic of your survey and the requirements for participation, including a statement indicating that participation is voluntary and that the participant is free to withdraw at any time.

3. A statement that all data will be held in confidence and that the data will be used only within the Research Methods class for educational purposes.

4. An acknowledgment that the participant understands the nature and purpose of the study, that he/she is at least 18 years old, and that the participant freely consents to participate.

III. Administering Your Questionnaire

Each person in your lab group will administer the questionnaire to at least five people. Work out within your lab group precisely how the questionnaire is to be administered by members of your group.

IV. Analysis

Your questionnaire data will be evaluated along the following lines:

1. You will obtain an overall score on the questionnaire by summing over all items on your questionnaire. Before you do this, be sure to rekey your negatively keyed items so that they are positively keyed. That is, assign strongly disagree = 5, disagree = 4, and so on.

2. Descriptive statistics will be computed for the overall score as well as for each item separately.

3. The reliability of your questionnaire will be evaluated by applying *coefficient alpha,* which is defined by the following formula (Anastasi, 1976):

$$r_\alpha = \frac{n}{n-1} \cdot \frac{s_t^2 - \Sigma s_i^2}{s_t^2}$$

where n is the number of items on the questionnaire, s_t^2 is the variance (SD^2 for the total) for the entire questionnaire, and Σs_i^2 is the sum of the individual item variances (SD^2 for each item).

4. An item analysis will be conducted by computing the Pearson correlation between the scores on each item and the overall score on the questionnaire. For example, each subject will have a score on each item as well as an overall score. For each item you will take the score on a particular item and the overall score for each subject and enter those scores into a Pearson correlation analysis. The higher the correlation, the more "internally valid" (or the better) the item. Items with a low correlation will have to be reworded or replaced.

5. Correlations between your "predictor" items and the overall attitude score will be computed to see if there are any subject characteristics that correlate with the attitude measured.

Sampling Demonstration

Students often have a difficult time understanding how a simple random sample can produce data that are (usually) representative of the population. An effective way to bring home this fact is to conduct a small-scale demonstration using the class as the population and drawing random samples of a given size from the class. Consecutively number the students according to their seating positions, calling out the numbers so that each student knows his or her number (ask them to write it down; they forget). Then have one of the students use the table of random numbers in the back of the text to collect a random sample of, say, five students. Have the selected students come to the front of the class and have them measure each other on some interval or ratio scale variable, such as height, weight, or other variable that is interesting and convenient to measure. Write each value down and calculate the average of these values. Repeat the whole procedure for five samples (with replacement).

At this point, you can note that each sample represents an independent "best guess" as to the population mean. Note how these means compare. Note that sometimes the mean of a sample will not agree well with the means of the other samples. You can point out that such samples, although random, may not be representative of the population, but that according to the laws of probability, most sample means will be fairly close to the population value.

Now average the sample means. Finally, measure all remaining students on the variable of interest and calculate the mean for the population. Generally, this will be close to the population value. You could point out at this time that the mean of the means of all possible samples of a given size from the population exactly equals the population value (central limit theorem).

If you had a discrepant sample mean, you could use this example to note that random sampling does not *guarantee* a representative sample, but does assure that most samples will be representative to a reasonable degree, and that, furthermore, by using a random sample, you can estimate the probability that any given sample will be deviant.

Participating in an Internet Survey

Have students find an ongoing survey study on the Internet. These can easily be found through Yahoo <http://www.yahoo.com> by clicking first on Science, then on Psychology, and then on Tests and Experiments. They will find a list of studies being conducted on the Internet, some of which will be surveys. Have each person choose one of the surveys and participate in it. Have them note whether the survey is one that is conducted directly online or one where a survey form is e-mailed to them. Have each student note the topic of the survey, the format of the questionnaire, the types of items used, its organization. Discuss your students' experiences in class. Focus on issues such as questionnaire design and the issues relating to sampling discussed in Chapter 7.

CHAPTER 8

USING BETWEEN-SUBJECTS AND WITHIN-SUBJECTS EXPERIMENTAL DESIGNS

KEY QUESTIONS TO CONSIDER

- How do between-subjects, within-subjects, and single-subject experiments differ?
- How might error variance in a between-subjects design affect your results and what steps can be taken to handle it?
- How are statistics used to test the reliability of data from a between-subjects experiment?
- How does a randomized group experiment work? What are some of its advantages and disadvantages?
- When would you use a matched-groups design?
- How does a matched-pairs design differ from a matched-groups design?
- What are some of the advantages and disadvantages of the matching strategy?
- What are some of the advantages and disadvantages of within-subjects designs?
- How do carryover effects influence interpretation of the results from a within-subjects experiment?
- Under what conditions will counterbalancing be effective or ineffective in dealing with carryover effects?
- When do you use a Latin square design?
- What steps can you take to handle carryover effects?
- Do between-subjects and within-subjects designs applied to the same variables always produce the same functional relationships?
- When should you consider using a within-subjects design over a between-subjects design?
- When should you consider using a matched-groups design rather than a within-subjects design?
- How do single-factor and multiple-factor designs differ and why would you use a multiple-factor design?
- What is a main effect and how does it differ from an interaction?
- How does a confounding variable affect the validity of your results and how can confounding be eliminated?

CHAPTER OUTLINE

Types of Experimental Design
The Problem of Error Variance in Between-Subjects and Within-Subjects Designs
    Sources of Error Variance
    Handling Error Variance
        Reducing Error Variance
        Increasing the Effectiveness of Your Independent Variable
        Randomizing Error Variance Across Groups
        Statistical Analysis
Between-Subjects Designs
    The Single-Factor Randomized Groups Design
        The Randomized Two-Group Design
        The Randomized Multigroup Design
    Matched Groups Designs
        Logic of the Matched Groups Design
        Advantages and Disadvantages of the Matched Groups Design

KEY TERMS

Between-subjects design	Matched pairs design
Within-subjects design	Carryover effects
Single-subject design	Counterbalancing
Error variance	Latin square design
Randomized two-group design	Factorial design
Parametric design	Main effect
Nonparametric design	Interaction
Multiple control group design	Higher order factorial design
Matched groups design	

CHAPTER GOALS

Chapter 8 is the first chapter on experimental designs and therefore includes a brief overview of the three main types of experimental design: between-subjects, within-subjects, and single-subject. This is followed by a description of the logic underlying between-subjects designs, including sources of variance and how between-subjects designs deal with them. The bulk of the chapter is taken up by descriptions of the various types of between-subjects and within-subjects designs, including single-factor randomized groups designs, matched groups and pairs designs, various within-subjects designs (including two-level and multilevel), factorial designs, and multivariate designs. The chapter closes with a discussion of confounding. When they have completed Chapter 8, students should know

- The defining characteristics of between-subjects, within-subjects, and single-subject designs.
- The sources of error variance in experimental designs and how error variance is handled (reducing error variance, increasing effectiveness of the independent variable, and statistical analysis).
- The characteristics of the single-factor, two-group randomized design.
- The limitations of the single-factor, two-group design.
- How the basic two-group randomized design can be expanded.
- The distinction between parametric and nonparametric multigroup experiments.
- The logic behind matching and the strategies involved in the matched groups and matched pairs designs.
- The defining characteristics of the within-subjects design along with its advantages and disadvantages.
- The problem of carryover effects and the strategies used to deal with carryover.
- When within-subjects designs should be used.
- The single-factor within-subjects designs (two-level and multilevel designs).
- The basic logic behind designs with two or more independent variables (factorial designs).
- The distinction between main effects and interactions.
- Higher order between-subjects and within-subjects designs.
- What it means to say that a design is multivariate.
- What confounding is and some ways in which it can creep into a design.

IDEAS FOR CLASS ACTIVITIES

Imagery and Recall

The following is a handout we give our students that provides the materials and method for a 2×2 factorial between-subjects design. The factors manipulated are (a) instructions to use imagery or rote memorization (Instruction Type) and (b) presentation of concrete or abstract words (Word Type). The two variables are so powerful that they are almost certain to produce good results, including a significant interaction. This provides a nice opportunity to show students what an interaction is and how it can be interpreted.

Imagery and Recall Experiment

For our next lab project we will be conducting an experiment on the relationship between imagery and recall. Research has shown that imagery tends to facilitate memory processes. In this experiment we will test this idea.

Design

This lab project will illustrate a two-factor, completely between-subjects experimental design. There are two factors: Instruction Type (Imagery Versus Rehearsal) and Word Type (Concrete and Abstract). Hence this experiment is a 2×2 factorial.

Participants

Each of you will be responsible for finding and running *FOUR* participants (one in each of the experimental conditions).

Materials

The materials for this experiment will be an informed consent form (to be supplied), the instructions to be read to participants (see attached page), and two lists of words, one consisting of concrete nouns and the other consisting of abstract nouns (see attached lists). Additionally, each participant will be provided with a response sheet.

Procedure

Participants are to be approached and asked if they would mind taking part in a simple experiment on memory. If the participant agrees, find a quiet place to conduct the experiment. Give the participant an informed consent form and read the form to him or her. After reading the informed consent form, have the participant sign and date it and return it to you. Next, read to the participant the appropriate instructions and read the list of word pairs. The list should be read at a rate of *ONE WORD PAIR EVERY 15 SECONDS* in all conditions.

After reading the list to the participants, go back and read each *STIMULUS WORD* to the participant and have him or her write down the appropriate response word on the response sheet. Read the list of stimulus words at a rate of one every 15 seconds.

Note: Each "experimenter" must run one participant in each of the experimental conditions. So, each of you will run a participant in the imagery/high-imagery words, imagery/low-imagery words, rehearsal/high-imagery words, and rehearsal/low-imagery words conditions.

Instructions: Imagery Group

This experiment concerns how well you can remember words. I will read you a list of word pairs (for example: water–bird). After I have read the entire list to you, I will give you the first word from each pair (for example, water) and you will give me the word that was paired with it (for example, bird). Also, I will be giving you the first word from each pair in an order that is different from the order in which the list will be read originally. So, don't try to remember the word pairs in order.

When you are trying to learn the word pairs, try to form a mental image (picture) of the two words going together. For example, if the word pair was water–bird, you might form the image of a bird sitting in a pool of water. Try to form such an image for each word pair.

Are there any questions?

Are you ready to begin?

Instructions: Rehearsal Group

This experiment concerns how well you can remember words. I will read you a list of word pairs (for example: water–bird). After I have read you the entire list, I will give you the first word from each pair (for example, water) and you will give me the word that was paired with it (for example, bird). Also, I will be giving you the first word from each pair in an order that is different from the order in which the list will be read originally. So, don't try to remember the word pairs in order.

When you are trying to learn the word pairs, say each word pair over and over to yourself. For example, if the word pair was water–bird, you would say water–bird, water–bird, water–bird, and so on until I read you the next word pair. Rehearse each word pair in this way.

Are there any questions?

Are you ready to begin?

HIGH-IMAGERY LIST

Stimulus word	Response word
POTATO	ROPE
BASKET	FLOWER
BELL	PRISON
STUDENT	BOTTLE
TICKET	COFFEE
BREAKFAST	APPLE
LIBRARY	DIAMOND
PALACE	TOWER
PIE	STAMP
SAILOR	TONGUE
FUR	MAGAZINE
FACTORY	FURNITURE

LOW-IMAGERY LIST

Stimulus word		Response word
ANGER	-->	BURDEN
BOND	-->	BREATH
LIBERTY	-->	EFFECT
AID	-->	HABIT
JUSTICE	-->	OWNER
ADVENTURE	------------------------------->	FAULT
SERIES	-->	HAPPINESS
PATTERN	-->	SECRET
SUM	-->	APPEARANCE
MASS	-->	EVIDENCE
CONTRACT	---------------------------------->	SIN
EVENT	-->	RELIEF

Order of Stimulus Words for Recall

HIGH-IMAGERY LIST

BREAKFAST
FACTORY
PALACE
STUDENT
SAILOR
POTATO
PIE
TICKET
FUR
BASKET
LIBRARY
BELL

LOW-IMAGERY LIST

LIBERTY
SUM
JUSTICE
AID
ADVENTURE
MASS
CONTRACT
EVENT
ANGER
PATTERN
BOND
SERIES

Experimental Design With Codes

WORD TYPE

	HIGH-IMAGERY	LOW-IMAGERY
IMAGERY	1	2
REHEARSAL	3	4

(INSTRUCTION)

Informed Consent Form

This experiment is being conducted as a class project for Research Methods under the direction and guidance of the instructor of the course. It deals with your ability to recall a list of words. If you agree to participate, I will read you a list of word pairs. I will then give you the first word from each pair and you will have to recall the word that goes with it. The experiment should only take a few minutes of your time.

Your participation in this experiment is voluntary and you are free to withdraw at any time without penalty, and remove any data that you may have contributed.

Please be assured that at no time will your name be reported along with your responses. In fact, this informed consent form will be kept separate from your responses. Also, your participation in this study is confidential, as are any responses that you give. Also, the responses that you provide will be used within the Research Methods class for the purposes of learning about research methodology and will not be reported outside of the class.

I acknowledge that I am at least 18 years old and that the purposes and procedures of this experiment have been explained to me to my satisfaction. I understand that my participation in this study is totally voluntary and that I am free to withdraw at any time with no penalty. Knowing the above I freely consent to participate.

Signed _____

Date _____

Response Sheet

After I read the first word from each word pair, please write down the second word.

1. _____   7. _____
2. _____   8. _____
3. _____   9. _____
4. _____   10. _____
5. _____   11. _____
6. _____   12. _____

Code _____

Sexual Harassment Experiment

The issue of sexual harassment has become a hot political issue, and as a consequence a hot area of research. Below is a set of materials that you can use to conduct a simple 2×2 between-subjects factorial experiment. The two independent variables are: the status differential between two parties involved in an alleged harassment incident (equal [two students] or unequal [student–professor] and frequency of the harassment incident [once; several times]).

Reproduce enough of the materials so that you can have your students run the experiment. Have students run an equal number of male and female participants. Sex will be included as a quasi-independent variable to determine if males and females perceive incidents of alleged sexual harassment differently. After the data are collected, have your students summarize them with descriptive statistics and perform the appropriate inferential statistical test (a between-subjects ANOVA). Have each student prepare a lab report or a full APA-style paper reporting the methods, results, and conclusions.

We have provided an informed consent form that you may modify to fit your needs. Simply substitute your university's name, your name and department name, and where and when a copy of results may be obtained in the places indicated.

Variations

You can easily modify these materials to include a third variable (e.g., gender of the victim, the severity of the harassment incident [a professor helping a student with her schoolwork only if she agrees to go on a date with him; showing a picture of a nude painting in an art history book]). You can add or delete measures. The possibilities are limitless.

References

Here are a few references to get you and your students started on a literature search.

Bartling, C. A., & Eisenman, R. (1993). Sexual harassment proclivities in men and women. *Bulletin of the Psychonomic Society, 31,* 189–192.

Brusik, K. (1992). Perceptions of sexual harassment in an academic context. *Sex Roles, 27,* 401–412.

Kanekar, S., & Dhir, V. (1993). Sex-related differences in perceptions of sexual harassment of women in India. *Journal of Social Psychology, 133,* 119–120.

Marks, M. A., & Nelson, E. S. (1993). Sexual harassment on campus: Effects of professor gender on perception of sexually harassing behaviors. *Sex Roles, 28,* 207–217.

Tata, J. (1993). The structure and phenomenon of sexual harassment: Impact of category of sexually harassing behavior, gender, and hierarchical level. *Journal of Applied Social Psychology, 23,* 199–211.

Informed Consent Form

This experiment is designed to investigate how people perceive situations involving alleged sexual harassment. The experiment is being conducted as a requirement for a Research Methods class at [Insert your university]. The experiment is under the supervision of [Insert your name and department name].

For this experiment you will be asked to read a short scenario involving two individuals, one of whom filed a sexual harassment complaint against the other. After reading the scenario you will be asked to complete several measures relating to the scenario.

Please understand that your participation in this experiment is totally voluntary and that you are free to withdraw at any time during the experiment without penalty. You may remove any data that you contributed if you choose to withdraw. Also understand that all of your responses will be held in strict confidence by the experimenter. At no time will your name be reported along with your results. All results will be reported in group form only. Additionally, you may pick up a copy of the results of this experiment [Insert date and place where participants can pick up a copy of the results].

I acknowledge that I am at least 18 years of age and that the nature and requirements for participation in this experiment have been explained to me. Knowing these requirements, I freely consent to participate in this experiment.

Signed _____

Date _____

Instructions

This experiment is designed to investigate how people perceive incidents of alleged sexual harassment. Enclosed is a brief scenario for you to read depicting an interaction between two individuals, one of whom claims sexual harassment. After reading the scenario, you shall complete several measures relating to the scenario. Some of these measures ask you to circle a number on a rating scale. For these, simply circle the number on the scale that best reflects how you feel. Please follow the instructions given for completing each measure.

Are there any questions?

Before we begin, please provide the following information:

1. Your gender: _____ Male   _____ Female

2. Your current standing at the university:

    _____ First year

    _____ Second year

    _____ Third year

    _____ Fourth year

    _____ Not a university student

3. Your age _____

4. Your occupation _____

Experimental Condition: Equal Status; Single Incident

Sandra is a 19-year-old college sophomore. The following incident happened to her. One day after class a fellow student offered to help her get a better grade in the class, but only if she would agree to go out on a date with him. Sandra was offended by this student's behavior and filed a grievance against him with the University Review Board for sexual harassment. The review board agreed to hear her case.

Based on this scenario, please complete the following items:

1. To what extent does Sandra's fellow student's behavior constitute sexual harassment? (Circle the number that best reflects your judgment.)

    1 --------2---------3---------4---------5---------6---------7---------8---------9--------10
    Not at all   Somewhat   Very much

2. How reasonable do you think Sandra's action was in this case? (Circle the number that best reflects your judgment.)

    1 --------2---------3---------4---------5---------6---------7---------8---------9--------10
    Not at all   Somewhat   Very
    reasonable   reasonable   reasonable

3. Please describe the reason(s) why you felt that this incident did or did not constitute sexual harassment.

Experimental Condition: Unequal Status; Single Incident

Sandra is a 19-year-old college sophomore. The following incident happened to her. One day after class her professor offered to help her get a better grade in the class, but only if she would agree to go out on a date with him. Sandra was offended by this professor's behavior and filed a grievance against him with the University Review Board for sexual harassment. The review board agreed to hear her case.

Based on this scenario, please complete the following items:

1. To what extent does Sandra's professor's behavior constitute sexual harassment? (Circle the number that best reflects your judgment.)

   1 ---------2 ---------3 ---------4 ---------5 ---------6 ---------7 ---------8 ---------9 --------10
   Not at all   Somewhat   Very much

2. How reasonable do you think Sandra's action was in this case? (Circle the number that best reflects your judgment.)

   1 ---------2 ---------3 ---------4 ---------5 ---------6 ---------7 ---------8 ---------9 --------10
   Not at all   Somewhat   Very
   reasonable   reasonable   reasonable

3. Please describe the reason(s) why you felt that this incident did or did not constitute sexual harassment.

Experimental Condition: Equal Status; Several Incidents

Sandra is a 19-year-old college sophomore. The following incident happened to her. On several occasions after class a fellow student offered to help her get a better grade in the class, but only if she would agree to go out on a date with him. Sandra was offended by this student's behavior and filed a grievance against him with the University Review Board for sexual harassment. The review board agreed to hear her case.

Based on this scenario, please complete the following items:

1. To what extent does Sandra's fellow student's behavior constitute sexual harassment? (Circle the number that best reflects your judgment.)

   1 ---------2 ---------3 ---------4 ---------5 ---------6 ---------7 ---------8 ---------9 --------10
   Not at all   Somewhat   Very much

2. How reasonable do you think Sandra's action was in this case? (Circle the number that best reflects your judgment.)

   1 ---------2 ---------3 ---------4 ---------5 ---------6 ---------7 ---------8 ---------9 --------10
   Not at all   Somewhat   Very
   reasonable   reasonable   reasonable

3. Please describe the reason(s) why you felt that this incident did or did not constitute sexual harassment.

Experimental Condition: Unequal Status; Several Incidents

Sandra is a 19-year-old college sophomore. The following incident happened to her. On several occasions after class her professor offered to help her get a better grade in the class, but only if she would agree to go out on a date with him. Sandra was offended by this professor's behavior and filed a grievance against him with the University Review Board for sexual harassment. The review board agreed to hear her case.

Based on this scenario, please complete the following items:

1. To what extent does Sandra's professor's behavior constitute sexual harassment? (Circle the number that best reflects your judgment.)

   1 ---------2 ---------3 ---------4 ---------5 ---------6 ---------7 ---------8 ---------9 --------10
   Not at all   Somewhat   Very much

2. How reasonable do you think Sandra's action was in this case? (Circle the number that best reflects your judgment.)

1 --------- 2 --------- 3 --------- 4 --------- 5 --------- 6 --------- 7 --------- 8 --------- 9 ------- 10
Not at all   Somewhat   Very
reasonable   reasonable   reasonable

3. Please describe the reason(s) why you felt that this incident did or did not constitute sexual harassment.

Two-Factor Within-Subjects Experiment

The following describes a 2 × 2 factorial within-subjects experiment patterned after the classic Peterson and Peterson (1959) study of short-term memory. In the original experiment, subjects were given a consonant trigram, immediately followed by a three-digit number. Participants were instructed to successively subtract by 3 or 4, beginning with this number, until a light came on. The onset of the light was their cue to recall the trigram aloud to the experimenter. The retention interval (delay between receipt of the trigram and light onset) was manipulated within subjects between 3 and 18 seconds in 3-s increments.

We modified this experiment by including only the highest and lowest retention intervals and adding a second factor, the nature of the trigram (triple consonants or three-letter word) to form a 2 × 2 factorial manipulation. Stimulus presentation and interval timing were handled by computer in our experiment, but a simple timer or stopwatch could be used instead.

Effects of Retention Interval and Stimulus Meaningfulness
on Short-Term Memory for Trigrams

Participants

Participants can be members of the class or people recruited by the students. If class members are used, each student should serve once as participant and once as experimenter.

Materials

Each experimenter should have a stopwatch and four 20-item lists: two of three-letter words and two of CCCs (consonant-consonant-consonant trigrams). Each word or CCC should be paired with a three-digit number. On the same line, there should be a space for the participant's response to the item. Participants should be tested in isolated cubicles, if possible, to minimize disturbances and prevent participants from hearing items being presented to other participants. Have your students create a set of instructions to be read to the participants and an informed consent form. Each experimenter should then be given a copy of the instructions and one copy of the consent form for each participant he or she will test.

The instructions should inform the participants that the experiment is being conducted to assess their ability to remember information for brief periods of time. The participant will be given a series of stimulus items (words or consonant trigrams), each followed by a three-digit number. When the participant hears the number, he or she should repeat the number, then subtract 3 from it and give the result, then subtract 3 from the result, and so on, and continue until the experimenter says "STOP!" The participant should then attempt to recall the stimulus item given at the beginning of the trial.

STIMULUS LISTS

1.	DOG	FAN	DRW	TVC
2.	PEN	ELF	YPP	RST
3.	HAT	CAT	NPT	RHM
4.	PIG	WAR	LXV	YJL
5.	FLY	NET	NMF	NQG
6.	MAN	HEN	PYQ	PSM
7.	BAT	MAP	DZQ	QSW
8.	CAR	JAR	NXL	DPK
9.	SEA	APE	NMD	YSP
10.	HAM	EGG	RMK	FTP
11.	BOY	MAT	FNC	KPZ
12.	LET	POT	LTG	GTS
13.	SKY	RAT	KHP	VDB
14.	GUN	DEN	DKW	XMG
15.	ANT	RUG	LCH	KJQ
16.	AGE	ZOO	NRY	KGM
17.	LOG	NUT	YJY	MCT
18.	SUN	PAN	JRY	SYH
19.	BAR	ARM	CFS	VPW
20.	JET	TOE	DFH	XVJ

Procedure

The experimenter and participant should be seated facing one another, and should arrange the situation so that the participant cannot see the items on the lists (for example, by placing the lists in a clipboard). One word list and one CCC list are used for the 3-s retention interval; the other word and CCC lists are used for the 18-s retention interval. This yields four treatments: Word/3-s, Word/18-s, CCC/3-s, and CCC/18-s. The order in which these treatments are presented should be counterbalanced across participants. In addition, a given list should be associated with the 3-s interval for half the participants and with the 18-s interval for the other half to prevent confounding by list difficulty.

The experimenter should read the informed consent form to the participant and then have the participant sign the form. Next, the experimenter should read the instructions and ask the participant whether he or she understands what is required. If the participant is confused, the experimenter should then explain the procedure until the participant understands it.

The experimenter should then make sure the participant is ready to begin. When the participant is ready, the experimenter should read the first stimulus word or CCC from the first list, enunciating clearly, followed immediately by the number that is paired with the stimulus item. As the number is read, the stopwatch should be started.

Receipt of the number is the participant's cue to start subtracting out loud by 3s from the number. The participant should continue until the experimenter says "STOP!" and then should attempt to recall the stimulus item. The experimenter should record the participant's response and indicate whether it was correct or incorrect.

For one of the word lists and one of the CCC lists, the experimenter should say STOP when 3 seconds have elapsed on the stopwatch. For the other two lists (word and CCC) the experimenter should say STOP when 18 seconds have elapsed. The stopwatch should then be stopped and reset.

The experimenter should continue through the 20-item list and then give the participant a short "breather" before starting the next list, to reduce the effects of fatigue.

Analysis

The results should be analyzed with a two-factor within-subjects ANOVA. Have students create a line graph of the group means and discuss the results in class.

CHAPTER 9

USING SPECIALIZED RESEARCH DESIGNS

KEY QUESTIONS TO CONSIDER

- What is a mixed design and when is it used?
- What is a nested design and when is it used?
- What are the various types of nesting that can be done? Why might you use each?
- When would you consider using a design that combines experimental and correlational components?
- What is the definition of a quasi-independent variable?
- What are the advantages and disadvantages of including a quasi-independent variable in your experimental design?
- What are the characteristics of the time series designs and equivalent time samples design?
- What are the advantages and disadvantages of quasi-experimental designs?
- How are problems of internal validity addressed in a quasi-experimental design?
- What is the nonequivalent control group design? What are its strengths and weaknesses?
- What are the defining characteristics of the pretest–posttest design and what are some of the design's advantages and disadvantages?
- What is a Solomon four-group design and why would you consider using it?
- What are the defining qualities of the cross-sectional developmental design?
- What are the advantages and disadvantages of the cross-sectional design?
- What is a longitudinal developmental design?
- What are the advantages and disadvantages of the longitudinal design?
- What are the defining characteristics of the cohort-sequential developmental design?
- What are the advantages and disadvantages of the cohort-sequential design?

CHAPTER OUTLINE

Combining Between-Subjects and Within-Subjects Designs
    The Mixed Design
    The Nested Design
        Nesting Tasks
        Nesting Groups of Subjects
Combining Experimental and Correlational Designs
    Including a Covariate in Your Experimental Design
    Including Quasi-Independent Variables in an Experiment
        Advantages of Including a Quasi-Independent Variable
        Disadvantages of Including a Quasi-Independent Variable
Quasi-Experimental Designs
    Time Series Designs
        Interrupted Time Series Design
        Basic Data for Time Series Studies
    Equivalent Time Samples Design
    Advantages and Disadvantages of Quasi-Experiments
    Nonequivalent Control Group Design

KEY TERMS

Mixed design	Equivalent time samples design
Nested design	Nonequivalent control group design
Covariate	Pretest–posttest design
Quasi-independent variable	Solomon four-group design
Quasi-experimental design	Cross-sectional design
Time series design	Longitudinal design
Interrupted time series design	Cohort-sequential design

CHAPTER GOALS

This is the last of the chapters focusing on conventional experimental designs. Chapter 9 introduces students to a variety of specialized designs including mixed designs, covariate designs, quasi-experimental designs, pretest–posttest designs, and developmental designs. These designs are used when a research question cannot be adequately addressed with a straightforward experimental or correlational design.

When covering the combined experimental/correlational designs, you should emphasize the fact that the correlational variable in such a design cannot be interpreted in the same way as the experimental variable (a causal role can be deduced only for the experimental variable). Because experimental and quasi-experimental variables look the same to ANOVA, even professional researchers sometimes fail to keep the distinction in mind, but it is important that they (and your students) do so.

Major points to cover in your lectures might include the following:

- What a mixed design is and when to use it.
- What a nested design is, how nesting can be done, and when the design is used.
- The difference between a mixed and nested design.
- How to combine experimental and correlational designs.
- Including a covariate in an experimental design to statistically control the effects of extraneous variables.
- How to interpret results relating to the experimental and correlational variables in the design combining experimental and correlational components.
- The definition of a quasi-experimental variable.
- The advantages and disadvantages of including quasi-independent variables in a design.
- The defining characteristics of the time series and interrupted time series design.
- The defining characteristics of the equivalent time samples design.
- The advantages and disadvantages of quasi-experimental designs.
- What a nonequivalent control group design is used for.
- What pretest–posttest designs are, what they are for, and how to deal with potential problems created by the pretest.
- The characteristics of the cross-sectional developmental design along with its advantages and disadvantages.

- The characteristics of the longitudinal developmental design along with its advantages and disadvantages.
- The characteristics of the cohort-sequential developmental design along with its advantages and disadvantages.

IDEAS FOR CLASS ACTIVITIES

Mixed Experiment

The classic mixed experiment combines a between-subjects variable with a repeated measure across trials. In this experiment we examine the effects of Memorization Technique and Number of Trials on recall of a list of words. Recall is assessed on each trial by using the paired-associates technique.

Subjects

Subjects should be randomly assigned into two groups, preferably in equal numbers.

Materials

If you have access to a memory drum or computer, you can use these devices to present the stimuli at a uniform rate. However, a simple watch that provides the seconds and 3 inch × 5 inch cards will perform satisfactorily. Print the stimulus word on one side of the card and both the stimulus word and response word on the other side, separated by a dash. For the computer or memory drum, present the stimulus word, then the paired stimulus-response words at an even rate (see Procedure). Here is a list of 20 paired associates to use:

1. DOG–TREE	11. HAMMER–CARROT
2. POTATO–SHOE	12. PUMPKIN–HOUSE
3. BALLOON–PHONE	13. FLOWER–HAT
4. CLOCK–COMPUTER	14. WAGON–LAMP
5. ONION–LIPSTICK	15. STRING–PAPER
6. DESK–ROCK	16. GREASE–TOOTHBRUSH
7. BOOK–SHELF	17. BASEBALL–RACQUET
8. TRUCK–MILK	18. CHICKEN–BRIEFCASE
9. BAG–BOTTLE	19. TROMBONE–HOSE
10. DRUM–PERFUME	20. SOAP–GLASSES

Procedure

The between-subjects variable, Memorization Technique, has two levels corresponding to the two groups: Visualization and Rehearsal. Participants in the Visualization group receive the following instructions:

> In a moment you will be shown a series of stimulus words. Each stimulus word will paired with a response word. Try to form a vivid and silly visual image that incorporates both words. For example, if the two words were Horse–Man, you might picture a horse riding a man, complete with saddle.
>
> After you have seen all the stimulus-response pairs, you will then be shown the stimulus words, one at a time. As you see each word, try to recall your visual image. Then tell your experimenter what you think the response word is. If you do not know, take a guess. When you have made your guess, the experimenter will show you the stimulus-response pair. Check to see whether your response was correct, and then form your visual image again.

The instructions for the Repetition group are as follows:

> In a moment you will be shown a series of stimulus words. Each stimulus word will paired with a response word. Repeat the stimulus-response pair to yourself until the experimenter removes the card.
>
> After you have seen all the stimulus-response pairs, you will then be shown the stimulus words, one at a time. As you see each stimulus word, try to recall the response word. Then tell your experimenter what you think the response word is. If you do not know, take a guess. When you have made your guess, the experimenter will show you the stimulus-response pair. Check to see whether your response was correct, and then repeat the stimulus-response pair to yourself until the experimenter removes the card.

Read the appropriate instructions to the participant and then ask the participant if he or she understands what is expected. (If the participant is confused, explain the procedure until he or she knows what to do). Then show each stimulus-response pair to the participant at a rate of one every 10 seconds. This completes the first trial.

On the second and subsequent trials, present the stimulus word and wait until the participant gives a response or 10 seconds elapse. Record whether the response to that stimulus word was correct (if no response was given, record it as incorrect), then show the participant the stimulus-response pair for 5 seconds. Then go on to the next stimulus word. Repeat this procedure for all 20 pairs. Then start over again and repeat until you have completed five test trials (or six trials in all).

Analysis

Tally the number of correct responses on each trial for each group. Then use LabStat or another statistical analysis package to create a data file and conduct a two-factor mixed ANOVA on the data. Create a graph with Trials on the x-axis and Number Correct on the y-axis, then plot the number correct for each group on each test trial (use circles for the Visualization group, squares for the Repetition group).

Combined Design Experiment

A simple between-subjects experiment can be converted to one that includes a quasi-independent variable simply by separating the subjects according to some subject characteristic. If your class includes a relatively even mix of males and females, you might consider using gender as the quasi-independent variable (failing to find a gender difference may be as interesting as finding one, especially if the dependent variable is associated with sexual stereotyping). Use the appropriate two-factor ANOVA to analyze the data, and then give students an opportunity to interpret the results. This can be a good time to reinforce the inappropriateness of attributing a causal role to the quasi-independent variable.

Developmental Research

Although it is not usually feasible to have students conduct a developmental study in a research methods class, you can still reinforce the points made in the text by having each student find a journal article illustrating each of the three developmental designs. Have the students analyze each article according to the guidelines provided in Chapter 2 of this manual. Have students pay special attention to the aspects of the study relevant to developmental designs (e.g., generation effects, subject mortality). Discuss with the class two or three representative articles, and show how each design was employed to evaluate age-related changes in behavior.

CHAPTER 10

USING SINGLE-SUBJECT DESIGNS

KEY QUESTIONS TO CONSIDER

- How were single-subject designs used in the early days of behavioral research?
- What are the major characteristics of the single-subject, baseline design?
- What is a behavioral baseline and why is it important in a single-subject baseline design?
- What are stability criterion, intrasubject replication, and intersubject replication?
- How does the baseline design differ from group-based designs?
- How does the baseline design handle random variability and error variance?
- How do you assess the reliability and the generality of findings from a single-subject baseline design?
- What strategies are used when implementing a baseline experiment?
- What are some of the problems faced when establishing baselines and how can these problems be handled?
- What are the characteristics of the single-factor, baseline design?
- How do multifactor baseline designs work?
- What is a multiple baseline design and when would you use one?
- What does it mean to observe behavioral dynamics?
- What are the major characteristics of the discrete-trials design?
- How are inferential statistics used in single-subject designs?
- What are the advantages and disadvantages of the single-subject approach?

CHAPTER OUTLINE

A Little History
Baseline Versus Discrete Trials Designs
Baseline Designs
    Features of the Baseline Design
        The Behavioral Baseline
        Stability Criterion
        Intrasubject Replication
        Intersubject Replication
    Rationale of the Baseline Design
        Dealing With Random Variability
        Handling Error Variance
        Assessing the Reliability of Findings
        Determining the Generality of Findings
    Implementing a Single-Subject Baseline Design
    Dealing With Problem Baselines
        Unsystematic Baseline Variability
        Drifting Baselines
        Unrecoverable Baselines
        Unequal Baselines Between Subjects
        Inappropriate Baseline Levels
    Types of Single-Subject Baseline Design

KEY TERMS

Baseline design	Error variance
Baseline phase	Systematic replications
Intervention phase	Direct replications
Behavioral baseline	Reversal strategy
Stability criterion	ABA design
Intrasubject replication	ABAB design
Intersubject replication	Multiple-baseline design
Systematic variance	Discrete trials design

CHAPTER GOALS

Chapter 10 introduces students to single-subject or small-*n* designs, which include both the baseline designs pioneered by B. F. Skinner and the older, discrete-trials type. A major goal of the chapter is to show how valid inferences about causal relationships can be drawn from single-subject data even though group-based statistical analyses cannot be performed. Instead, techniques such as rigid control over extraneous variables, use of stability criteria, and replication provide the means to uncover causal relationships and assess their reliability.

The chapter opens with a brief outline of the history of single-subject designs and then compares the baseline and discrete trials approaches. The characteristics of baseline designs are then described, including the behavioral baseline, stability criterion, intrasubject replication, and intersubject replication. The chapter then takes up the logic of the baseline design and takes students through an example implementation of the design. How to deal with problem baselines is then described, followed by a description of the major types of baseline design.

Discrete trials designs are introduced next and an example signal detection experiment is described. Some attempts to apply inferential statistics to single-subject data (using multiple observations in place of multiple subjects) are discussed and the problems noted. The chapter concludes with a summary of the advantages and disadvantages of the single-subject approach.

Suggested points to cover in your lecture include the following:

- The origins of the single-subject, or small-*n*, approach to research.
- The differences between the baseline and discrete trials designs.
- Contrast how reliability is assessed in the single-subject and group-based designs. You might point out that *both* types of design use replication to assess reliability. Group designs expose several subjects to the same treatment (replication across subjects), whereas single-subject designs expose one subject to each treatment repeatedly (replication across treatments).
- The role of the baseline in establishing a basis for comparison across treatments in the baseline design.
- The requirement in baseline designs of rigidly controlling extraneous variables in order to obtain stable baselines.
- How to establish a stability criterion and how the stability criterion is used in baseline designs.
- Conditions under which a simple baseline design cannot be used (e.g., irreversible effects).
- Advantages and disadvantages of single-subject designs.

- How to use baseline designs with more than two levels of an independent variable or more than one independent variable.
- The different types of baseline designs and their uses.
- How behavioral dynamics are observed and what they tell you about behavior.
- The logic of the discrete trials single-subject design.
- The major characteristics of the discrete trials design.
- How data from discrete trials designs are analyzed.
- Why standard inferential statistics cannot be used to analyze data from discrete trials single-subject designs.

IDEAS FOR CLASS ACTIVITIES

Single-Subject Baseline Experiment

If you have facilities available for conditioning rats or pigeons (and you can get the proper clearance from your local animal care and use committee), nothing beats a simple experiment involving reinforcement versus extinction, different reinforcement schedules, delay of reinforcement, or stimulus discrimination. Our students are always amazed to see their rats acquiring a lever-press response and demonstrating the behavioral patterns the students have previously only read about in their textbooks. You can use these experiments to demonstrate the establishment of a behavioral baseline, selection of a stability criterion, the changes in baseline that take place between treatment conditions, intrasubject replication, and intersubject replication.

Our procedure is to assign two students to a rat and operant chamber and have the students observe the animal and plot its response output over intervals of 5 minutes. We take care of properly depriving the rats prior to the lab session and magazine training the rat in the operant chamber. When the rat has acquired its response and the baseline has stabilized, the students switch the rat to the treatment condition. We normally use a simple ABAB design for the experiment.

When all the rats have completed all phases of the experiment, the students meet as a group and compare their graphs. This is a good time to talk about any difficulties some of the students may have encountered (failing to get response acquisition, erratic baselines, etc.) and to suggest possible causes and cures for these difficulties. When students compare their graphs, they are often surprised about how similar the performances of the different rats were to one another. We usually create a summary graph that includes the data that met the stability criterion. This makes it easy to examine the degree of intersubject replication.

Discrete Trials Experiment

We have used a number of discrete trials experiments in our lab with good results. Here is one of them.

Difference Threshold for Lifted Weight

This is a replication of Weber's classic lifted weight experiment using the method of constant stimuli. Each participant lifts a "standard" weight, followed by a "comparison" weight, and then tells the experimenter whether the comparison seemed heavier or lighter than the standard ("equal" is not an allowed response).

Materials

You will need to obtain 24 identical opaque plastic vials with screw caps and fill each vial with lead shot so as to obtain a series of weights as follows (in grams):

Standard	Comparisons
100 g	75, 80, 85, 90, 95, 100, 105, 110, 115, 120, 125 g
200 g	175, 180, 185, 190, 195, 200, 205, 210, 215, 220, 225 g

Stuff cotton over the shot to keep the shot from moving in the vial. Mark the weight of each vial on the bottom.

Make up a blindfold and an informed consent form for each participant. Make up two data sheets as follows:

Experimenter _____   Date _____

Participant _____

Coding: 0 = "lighter"   1 = "heavier"

					Comparison Weights						
Replic.	75	80	85	90	95	100	105	110	115	120	125
1	—	—	—	—	—	—	—	—	—	—	—
2	—	—	—	—	—	—	—	—	—	—	—
3	—	—	—	—	—	—	—	—	—	—	—
4	—	—	—	—	—	—	—	—	—	—	—
5	—	—	—	—	—	—	—	—	—	—	—
6	—	—	—	—	—	—	—	—	—	—	—
7	—	—	—	—	—	—	—	—	—	—	—
8	—	—	—	—	—	—	—	—	—	—	—
9	—	—	—	—	—	—	—	—	—	—	—
10	—	—	—	—	—	—	—	—	—	—	—
11	—	—	—	—	—	—	—	—	—	—	—
12	—	—	—	—	—	—	—	—	—	—	—
13	—	—	—	—	—	—	—	—	—	—	—
14	—	—	—	—	—	—	—	—	—	—	—
15	—	—	—	—	—	—	—	—	—	—	—
16	—	—	—	—	—	—	—	—	—	—	—
17	—	—	—	—	—	—	—	—	—	—	—
18	—	—	—	—	—	—	—	—	—	—	—
19	—	—	—	—	—	—	—	—	—	—	—
20	—	—	—	—	—	—	—	—	—	—	—
Total	—	—	—	—	—	—	—	—	—	—	—
Prop.	—	—	—	—	—	—	—	—	—	—	—

(Prop. = Proportion of "heavier" responses = Total/20.)

Experimenter _____   Date _____

Participant _____

Coding: 0 = "lighter"   1 = "heavier"

Comparison Weights

Replic.	175	180	185	190	195	200	205	210	215	220	225
1	___	___	___	___	___	___	___	___	___	___	___
2	___	___	___	___	___	___	___	___	___	___	___
3	___	___	___	___	___	___	___	___	___	___	___
4	___	___	___	___	___	___	___	___	___	___	___
5	___	___	___	___	___	___	___	___	___	___	___
6	___	___	___	___	___	___	___	___	___	___	___
7	___	___	___	___	___	___	___	___	___	___	___
8	___	___	___	___	___	___	___	___	___	___	___
9	___	___	___	___	___	___	___	___	___	___	___
10	___	___	___	___	___	___	___	___	___	___	___
11	___	___	___	___	___	___	___	___	___	___	___
12	___	___	___	___	___	___	___	___	___	___	___
13	___	___	___	___	___	___	___	___	___	___	___
14	___	___	___	___	___	___	___	___	___	___	___
15	___	___	___	___	___	___	___	___	___	___	___
16	___	___	___	___	___	___	___	___	___	___	___
17	___	___	___	___	___	___	___	___	___	___	___
18	___	___	___	___	___	___	___	___	___	___	___
19	___	___	___	___	___	___	___	___	___	___	___
20	___	___	___	___	___	___	___	___	___	___	___
Total	___	___	___	___	___	___	___	___	___	___	___
Prop.	___	___	___	___	___	___	___	___	___	___	___

(Prop. = Proportion of "heavier" responses = Total/20.)

Procedure

The participant is seated across from the experimenter at a small table. The experimenter should explain the nature of the experiment to the participant and then have the participant read and sign the informed consent form. The experimenter should then explain the procedure to the participant and make sure the participant understands the procedure. The procedure consists of the following:

The experimenter blindfolds the participant and then selects one of the two sets of weights. The standard weight from this set is placed in front of the participant. The participant is informed that this is the standard weight and is instructed to lift the weight and immediately put it back down. The participant should use whichever hand is most comfortable, but should always use the same hand for lifting the weights.

The experimenter then replaces the standard weight with one of the comparison weights from the same set, informs the participant that this is a comparison weight, and instructs the participant to lift this weight in the same way as the standard. The participant then announces "heavier" or "lighter" according to whether the comparison weight felt heavier or lighter than the standard weight. The experimenter records the participant's response on the data sheet, marking "0" for "lighter" and "1" for "heavier," and then replaces the comparison weight with the standard weight.

This procedure is repeated until the participant has compared the standard to each of the comparison weights. The entire set of comparisons is conducted 20 times, presenting the comparison weights in a different order each time. (Prior to the experimental session, you or the students should prepare a list giving the ordering of the weights for each set of comparisons.)

At this point, the participant is allowed to rest for a short while. The entire procedure is then repeated with the other set of weights.

Analysis

The student experimenter should total the responses in each column on the data sheet and then compute the proportion of "heavier" responses for each comparison weight by dividing each of the numbers by 20. The student should then make up two graphs, one for each weight set. Each graph should indicate the comparison weights along the x-axis and the proportion of "heavier" responses along the y-axis. After filling in the point for each comparison weight, the student should try to draw a smooth S-shaped curve through the points. The curve should pass through the .50 proportion at the value of the standard weight.

The student should now find the place where the .25 proportion passes through the line and then read from this point on the line down to the x-axis. This point is the lower limit. Repeating this procedure at the .75 proportion gives the upper limit. The difference threshold is then computed as follows:

$$\text{Difference threshold} = (\text{Upper limit} - \text{Lower limit})/2.$$

Weber's law holds that the ratio of the difference threshold (delta I) to the intensity of the stimulus (I) should be a constant within the limits of experimental error. That is,

$$\frac{\text{delta } I}{I} = k,$$

where k is the Weber constant. Have students compute k for the two standard weights (I is the mass of the standard weight in grams). Does Weber's law hold?

CHAPTER 11

DESCRIBING DATA

KEY QUESTIONS TO CONSIDER

- Why is it important to scrutinize your data using exploratory data analysis (EDA)?
- How do you organize your data in preparation for data analysis?
- What are the advantages and disadvantages of analyzing grouped and individual data?
- How do various types of graphs differ and when should each be used?
- How do negatively accelerated, positively accelerated, and asymptotic functional relationships differ?
- Why is it important to graph your data?
- How do you graph a frequency distribution as a histogram? As a stemplot?
- What should you look for when examining the graph of a frequency distribution, and why?
- How do the mode, median, and mean differ? Under what conditions would you use each?
- What measures of spread are available and when would you use each?
- What is the five-number summary and how can you represent it graphically?
- What do measures of association tell you?
- What factors affect the direction and magnitude of a correlation coefficient?
- What is linear regression and how is it used to analyze data?
- How are the regression weights and standard error used to interpret the results from a multiple regression analysis?

CHAPTER OUTLINE

Descriptive Statistics and Exploratory Data Analysis
Organizing Your Data
    Organizing Your Data for Computer Entry
        Entering Your Data
    Grouped Versus Individual Data
        Grouped Data
        Individual Data
        Using Grouped and Individual Data
Graphing Your Data
    Elements of a Graph
    Bar Graphs
    Line Graphs
        Shapes of Line Graphs
    Scatterplots
    Pie Charts
    The Importance of Graphing Data
        Showing Relationships Clearly
        Choosing Appropriate Statistics
The Frequency Distribution
    Displaying Distributions

KEY TERMS

Exploratory data analysis (EDA)	Range
Bar graph	Interquartile range
Line graph	Variance
Scatterplot	Standard deviation
Pie chart	Five-number summary
Frequency distribution	Boxplot
Histogram	Pearson product–moment correlation coefficient,
Stemplot	or Pearson *r*
Skewed distribution	Point-biserial correlation
Normal distribution	Spearman rank order correlation (*rho*)
Outliers	Linear regression
Resistant measures	Bivariate linear regression
Mode	Least squares regression line
Median	Regression weight
Mean	Standard error of estimate

CHAPTER GOALS

Chapter 11 briefly reviews descriptive statistics, including frequency distributions and measures of center, spread, association, and bivariate regression. Students should learn how scores from a study are organized, summarized, and graphed. Emphasize the importance of exploring the data (exploratory data analysis, or EDA) prior to conducting inferential statistical tests. In this regard, graphical techniques are especially important, so we have introduced some of the most useful, including the histogram, stemplot, and boxplot for displaying distributions, line graphs, bar graphs, and pie charts for displaying measures of center and (exclusively in the latter case) proportions or percentages, and scatterplots and multiple boxplots to display relationships. Each of the measures of center and spread should be covered (we have found that even those students who have recently taken statistics need a review of descriptive statistics, especially the variance and standard deviation). The characteristics and applications of each measure are discussed. The section on measures of association and related topics includes discussions of the most popular measures of correlation. Students should learn the characteristics and applications of each. Also, discuss with your students the factors that affect the direction and magnitude of the correlation coefficient. Emphasize the fact that the correlation coefficient cannot be interpreted as an index of the causal relationship between variables. Review the following points with your class:

- How to organize data on a data summary sheet. Stress the importance of providing a logical organization.
- The different ways of graphing data (histogram, line graph, etc.) and why it is important to graph data.
- The characteristics and applications of each of the measures of center. Discuss with your class how the characteristics of the distribution of scores affect the decision about which measure of center to use.
- The characteristics and applications of the measures of spread. Discuss how the characteristics of the distribution of scores affect each measure.
- The various measures of association, especially the Pearson product–moment correlation coefficient. Discuss how to interpret correlation coefficients, including their signs and magnitudes.
- The concept behind bivariate regression and prediction. Spend some time talking about the regression line, regression weights, and the standard error of estimate.

IDEAS FOR CLASS ACTIVITIES

Examples from the Literature

Have students go to the library and find two or three articles in scientific journals that report descriptive statistics and present the results graphically. Have them find articles that illustrate the use of various measures of center and spread and the different types of graphs. For each article, have students identify how the descriptive statistics were used and how the data were presented in the graph. Each student should also interpret the graph(s) found in each article (for example, the shape of distributions, the type of functional relationship shown). Ask students if they think the graphs make the results easier to understand.

Constructing a Frequency Distribution

To reinforce how to construct a frequency distribution, have each student measure the heights of five adults (friends or relatives serve nicely) and bring their data to class. Next, develop categories (for example, less than 5'0", 5'0" to 5'6", 5'7" to 6'0", and so on) and build a frequency distribution.

Deciding on Measures of Center and Spread

To illustrate how to choose measures of center and spread, present students with the following distributions of scores. Have them determine which measure of center and of spread would best describe each distribution.

	Distribution 1	Distribution 2	Distribution 3
	5	1	1
	3	2	3
	6	9	2
	4	1	2
	5	10	1
	7	2	4
	6	9	2
	2	7	10
	5	1	9
	6	10	10
	5	2	2
	4	9	9
$\bar{x}$	4.83	5.25	4.58
s	1.40	4.00	3.73
Median	5	4.50	2.50
Range	5	9	9
IQR	2	7.5	7.0

Distribution 1:   The mean and standard deviation are the best descriptive statistics. In this distribution there are no extreme scores, so the mean and standard deviation provide reasonable measures of center and spread.

Distribution 2:   Distribution 2 approaches a bimodal distribution. There are several low scores (1–2) and several high scores (7–10). The mean and standard deviation are not the best measures to use in this case. There is no one best value to represent center. Consequently, two modes should be derived and used to describe the distribution. The interquartile range is probably the best estimate of variability.

Distribution 3:   Distribution 3 is positively skewed, with most scores at the lower end of the scale. The median is the best measure of center in this case. The interquartile range provides the best estimate of spread.

Interpreting Pearson *r*

Chapter 11 discusses the Pearson product–moment correlation as the most widely used measure of bivariate correlation. The text also discusses how the value of *r* is affected by various factors. Following are four sets of scores your students can analyze with a Pearson *r*. Have students compute *r*s for each set of scores (perhaps using LabStat). Then, for each set, have them create a scattergram and determine whether Pearson *r* is the best index of correlation.

	Set 1			Set 2	
X	Y		X	Y	
1	2		3	4	
4	7		5	9	
2	3		4	9	
6	5		9	3	
4	7		10	4	
3	4		2	3	
5	4		1	2	
5	6		6	10	
7	7		5	10	
8	8		9	3	
6	7		10	2	
8	6		1	3	
9	10		6	9	
8	9		8	2	
1	3		2	3	

	Set 3			Set 4	
X	Y		X	Y	
1	7		1	10	
3	8		3	4	
2	6		7	9	
1	1		8	7	
3	4		5	7	
2	7		9	10	
2	8		10	10	
1	3		8	7	
2	1		9	8	
1	6		3	5	
3	4		1	3	
3	5		2	4	
2	10		5	7	
1	3		9	10	
1	8		8	8	

Set 1:   The Pearson r is appropriate for the data in set 1 ($r = .849$). An inspection of a scatterplot of these data shows that the relationship between the two sets of scores is linear with no outliers.

Set 2:   The Pearson r is not appropriate for the data in set 2 ($r = -.044$). An inspection of a scatterplot of these data shows that there is a curvilinear relationship between X and Y. Thus, Pearson r will underestimate the degree of relationship between these two variables.

Set 3:   The Pearson r is not appropriate for the data in set 3 ($r = .121$). The problem in this data set is that the range of scores for variable X is restricted compared to its range in the other sets (all values ranged between 1 and 3). Consequently, Pearson r will probably underestimate the degree of relationship between these variables.

Set 4:   The Pearson *r* is not appropriate for the data in set 4, as presented. Even though the value of *r* is relatively high (*r* = .657), the presence of an outlier (1, 10) in the data set results in a lower value of *r* than would appear to be true given the pattern shown on a scattergram for the other pairs of scores. You might have students delete the outlying pair and rerun the analysis.

Bivariate Regression

Use the four data sets to illustrate bivariate regression. Have students compute the necessary statistics and discuss the results with them. Point out how the results are influenced by the "flaws" in the three "flawed" data sets.

CHAPTER 12

USING INFERENTIAL STATISTICS

KEY QUESTIONS TO CONSIDER

- Why are sampling distributions important in inferential statistics?
- What is sampling error and why is it important to know about?
- What are degrees of freedom and how do they relate to inferential statistics?
- How do parametric and nonparametric statistics differ?
- What is the general logic behind inferential statistics?
- How are Type I and Type II errors related?
- What is the meaning of "statistical significance"?
- When should you use a two-tailed test?
- What are the assumptions underlying parametric statistics?
- Which parametric statistics would you use to analyze data from an experiment with two groups? Identify which test would be used for a particular type of design or data.
- Which parametric statistic is most appropriate for designs with more than one level of a single independent variable?
- When would you do a "planned" comparison versus an "unplanned" comparison, and why?
- What is the difference between a weighted and an unweighted means analysis? When would you use either?
- What is a "main effect" and an "interaction" and how are they analyzed?
- Under what conditions would you use a nonparametric statistic?
- What is meant by the "power" of a statistical test and what factors can affect it?
- Does a statistically significant finding always have practical significance?
- When are data transformations used?
- What are the alternatives to inferential statistics for evaluating the reliability of data?

CHAPTER OUTLINE

Inferential Statistics: Basic Concepts
    Sampling Distribution
    Sampling Error
    Degrees of Freedom
    Parametric Versus Nonparametric Statistics
The Logic Behind Inferential Statistics
    Statistical Errors
    Statistical Significance
    One-Tailed Versus Two-Tailed Tests
Parametric Statistics
    Assumptions Underlying a Parametric Statistic
    Inferential Statistics With Two Samples
    The t Test
        The t Test for Independent Samples
        The t Test for Correlated Samples
        Contrasting Two Groups: An Example From the Literature

KEY TERMS

Inferential statistics	t test for correlated samples
Standard error of the mean	z test for the difference between two proportions
Degrees of freedom	Analysis of variance (ANOVA)
Type I error	F ratio
Type II error	p value
Alpha level	Planned comparisons
Critical region	Unplanned comparisons
t test for independent samples	Per-comparison error

Familywise error	Power
Chi-square	Effect size
Mann–Whitney U test	Data transformation

CHAPTER GOALS

The major goal of Chapter 12 is to provide students with a review of inferential statistics. In our experience many students come into the research methods course with a weak understanding of inferential statistics, even if they have already taken a statistics course. The greatest areas of confusion center on the logic behind inferential statistics and how to interpret the results of statistical tests. We have also found that students really do not have a good grasp of what the statistical tables in the Appendix represent. Consequently, we wrote Chapter 12 to emphasize understanding of inferential statistics rather than how to compute them. After covering Chapter 12, your students should have a better understanding of the general logic behind inferential statistics and how to interpret the results obtained. The following are some areas to highlight in class:

- The notion of inferring population characteristics from samples. Reinforce the notion that inferential statistics are aids in decision making, the decision usually being whether the observed sample means represent the same or different underlying populations.
- Sampling error, degrees of freedom, and the distinction between parametric and nonparametric statistics.
- The difference between a one-tailed and a two-tailed test. This is a good place to review the concept of the sampling distribution of a statistic and the meaning of the critical values found in statistical tables.
- Review the *applications* and *interpretation* of the major parametric statistics. Point out the importance of having your data meet the underlying assumptions of each test.
- Describe the analysis of variance, especially the two-factor analysis. Many students have a great deal of trouble understanding what an interaction is and why we do not interpret main effects when one is present. Be sure to highlight the difference between planned and unplanned comparisons and the problem of familywise error when many means are compared.
- Cover the nonparametric statistics discussed in the chapter. Emphasize the applications of each statistic and how the results are interpreted.
- Discuss what the power of a statistical test is and the factors that affect it.
- Discuss with your class the difference between practical and statistical significance. Often students equate statistical significance with practical significance. Point out that even if a difference between means is significant at $p < .00000001$, it can still be a meaningless difference on a practical level.
- Students often do not know what the α-level adopted really means. They think that if something is significant at $p < .001$ it is more significant than at $p < .05$. This error in reasoning should be corrected with a discussion of the meaning of statistical significance.
- A brief discussion of alternatives to inferential statistics (especially replication) should be included in your lecture. This will reinforce the idea that inferential statistics are only a tool to help you decide whether your results are reliable.

IDEAS FOR CLASS ACTIVITIES

The Logic Behind Inferential Statistics

Chapter 12 makes the point that inferential statistics help you to decide whether, for example, observed sample means represent the same or different underlying populations. You can use the following demonstration in class to help students gain a better understanding of statistical decision making.

In Appendix II of this manual we provide numbers representing four populations, each having a different range of values. Construct samples (any size you want; 10 is good) by drawing numbers from the populations. (Keep track of which samples come from which populations.) Pair off the samples and give them to your class. Have your students compute a mean and standard deviation for each sample and then decide whether the samples come from the same or different populations.

Next have them conduct a t test for independent samples on each pair of samples and evaluate t for statistical significance. Have students note whether the observed t score is statistically significant and whether their conclusions based on the results of the statistical test agree with their evaluations made prior to doing the *t* test.

In class discuss the following points:

1. The notion of errors in decision making (Type I and II errors) and why they might be made.

2. How inferential statistics such as the *t* test help you make statistical decisions and minimize errors.

3. The meaning of a statistically significant finding.

4. How statistical tables are used and what they really are (sampling distributions showing the probability of obtaining scores of a given value from a random sample).

Computing and Evaluating a Between-Subjects ANOVA

As a review of ANOVA, you can have students compute an ANOVA (using LabStat or another statistical analysis program) and evaluate the significance of the findings. Next we have reproduced the data from a 4×2 factorial experiment conducted by Bordens and Horowitz (1986). The data and results from a LabStat analysis of these data are provided in Appendix III of this manual. Have students do the following:

1. Compute a two-factor, between-groups ANOVA.

2. Determine whether the main effects and interaction are statistically significant at $\alpha = 0.05$.

3. Conduct follow-up tests to determine the locus of the significant effects. (If your statistical package does not perform these tests, you can substitute *t* tests while using a more stringent level of significance (e.g., $\alpha = .01$) to compensate for probability pyramiding, but be sure to point out to students that in professional work they should really be using one of the post hoc tests specifically designed for this purpose.)

Discuss with your class the following points:

1. What the values in the ANOVA table represent and how they are used to determine statistical significance.

2. How to interpret a significant overall *F* ratio.

3. How to conduct follow-up post hoc tests and how to interpret the results.

4. The meaning of the two significant main effects in the light of a nonsignificant interaction.

Computing and Evaluating a Within-Subjects ANOVA

The previous exercise had students compute and evaluate a between-subjects ANOVA. This exercise has students compute and evaluate a within-subjects ANOVA.

In Chapter 9 we described a replication and extension of Peterson and Peterson's (1959) classic experiment on short-term memory. For this exercise have students compute a two-factor within-subjects ANOVA using a statistical package such as LabStat. The data and the results from a LabStat analysis of the data are provided in Appendix III of this manual.

Follow the guidelines suggested in the previous exercise for this one. There is one major difference between this exercise and the previous one: there is a significant two-way interaction. Use this opportunity to discuss with your class how to analyze the simple main effects of the interaction and why you do not interpret main effects when a significant interaction is present.

CHAPTER 13

REPORTING YOUR RESEARCH RESULTS

KEY QUESTIONS TO CONSIDER

- How do you set up a paper using APA writing style?
- What is the heading style used in an APA-style manuscript?
- What information is included on the title page, and in what order would you find that information (from the top to the bottom of the page)?
- What are the differences between a running head and a manuscript page header?
- What is an abstract and why is it so important?
- What information goes into an abstract and how long should an abstract be?
- What information is included in the introduction to an APA-style paper? How is the introduction organized?
- What information would you expect to find in the method section? Describe the various subsections of the method section.
- What would you expect to find in the results section of a manuscript?
- How is the results section formatted and how are statistics reported?
- How is the discussion section of a manuscript organized, and what would you expect to find in the discussion section?
- When do you include author notes and footnotes in an APA-style manuscript? Where should they be placed?
- How are tables used in an APA-style manuscript formatted? When are tables used?
- How is a page containing a figure set up? When are figures used?
- What is included in the reference list of an APA-style manuscript? Describe how a typical journal reference is formatted.
- What are the general rules for using numbers in the text of a manuscript?
- What is biased language and how can you avoid using it?
- Why are clarity of expression, organization, and style so important to consider when preparing a manuscript? What does each comprise?
- What are plagiarism and lazy writing and how can you avoid them?
- What is typically the sequence of events involved in submitting a paper for publication?
- What is the difference between an oral presentation and a poster session?

CHAPTER OUTLINE

APA Writing Style
Writing an APA-Style Paper
    Getting Ready to Type
        Formatting a Page
        Heading Structure
    The Title Page
        Title
        Author Name(s) and Affiliation(s)
        Running Head
    The Abstract
        Formatting the Abstract

KEY TERMS

Manuscript page header	Materials subsection
Running head	Procedure subsection
Abstract	Results section
Introduction	Discussion section
Method section	Reference section
Subjects subsection	Plagiarism
Participants subsection	Lazy writing
Apparatus subsection	Paper presentation

CHAPTER GOALS

Chapter 13 introduces students to writing research reports. The chapter begins by introducing students to the basics of APA writing style (we could not hope to cover all aspects of APA writing style in a single chapter). The student should learn how to set up an APA-style report, including all of the necessary sections from title page to references.

A section-by-section analysis tells what goes into each section and subsection, describes how to set up a table for data presentation, and shows how to properly prepare graphs.

The second major section of the chapter emphasizes the importance of clarity of expression, organization, and style. Students often do not pay enough attention to good writing practices and produce papers written in stilted "scientificese" (e.g., incomplete sentences describing a procedure). Reinforce the importance of constructing grammatically correct sentences and organizing those sentences into coherent paragraphs. Paragraphs should be organized into larger coherent sections. Also, emphasize to students the importance of handing in papers that have been adequately proofread and corrected. A section on plagiarism and lazy writing is presented to help students avoid those serious flaws in writing. Finally, a brief section on disseminating research results is included.

In class you should highlight the following points:

- How to set up an APA-style paper (proper margins, major sections, and so on).
- How to format the title page and abstract within APA guidelines. Emphasize that the abstract is a concise summary of the reported research. Spend some time on the abstract because in our experience students have a great deal of trouble with it.
- How to write an effective introduction. Highlight the general to specific organization of an introduction. Also reinforce the importance of a thorough, yet concise literature review and a clear statement of the research hypothesis.
- Discuss with your class the information that goes into each subsection of the method section. Emphasize that the information should be complete enough so that someone could replicate the study. Remind them to write in complete sentences in the method section.
- Review how statistics are reported in the results section and how data can be presented in tables or graphs.
- Show how a discussion section is organized from specific to general, beginning with a restatement of the research hypothesis and ending with broad implications of the findings.
- Discuss how to format references both in the body of the report and in the reference section. Emphasize that any citation appearing in the text must be included in the reference list. Remind students about properly citing secondary sources.
- Spend some class time reinforcing the points made in the section on clarity of expression, organization, and style. It does not hurt to keep reminding students that they should pay attention to grammatical correctness, proper word choice, and economy of expression. Additionally, point out the importance of organizing sentences and paragraphs coherently.
- Discuss the issue of biased language and how to avoid it. Remind students that they should proof their writing and eliminate instances of biased language.
- Define plagiarism and lazy writing and give examples of each. Convey that both are unacceptable.
- Briefly discuss the ways that research is disseminated via publication and presentations at professional meetings.

IDEAS FOR CLASS ACTIVITIES

Student Critiques

Students often have difficulty communicating their ideas clearly on paper, yet are unable to identify the flaws in their writing. This exercise allows students to critique each other's work, and can be carried out on lab reports or full APA-style papers.

Have students prepare and hand in two copies of a lab report or a full APA-style paper based on one of the research exercises carried out during the semester. Remove the title page from each copy and assign each paper a code number (perhaps the last four digits of the student's social security number) so that you can return the papers to their rightful owners. This technique amounts to a "masked review." Students may feel less inhibited about evaluating another person's work if the whole process is anonymous. Distribute the papers to the class, making sure that no student receives his or her own paper.

Have students evaluate and correct the papers by answering the following questions:

1. Are all of the sections and subsections of the paper in the proper order?
2. Within each section is all of the necessary information present (for example, are the subjects, materials, and procedures described fully)?

3. Within each section is the information presented in an organized, clear way? Are the paragraphs connected to one another logically? Are there any confusing, poorly written, or ambiguous sentences?

4. Are there any stylistic errors (for example, uncorrected typographical errors, misspelled words, improperly used words, glaring grammatical errors)?

5. Is there any evidence of biased language?

6. Are all the references given in the reference section cited in the paper? Conversely, are all references cited in the paper given in the reference section?

Poster Presentation

As a substitute for (or in addition to) preparing a written lab report or paper, have each student (or group of students if they work in groups) prepare a poster to present the results of one of the research projects done during the semester. The posters should include an abstract, introduction, method, results, discussion, and reference section. Have the students give a brief oral presentation of their project to the class.

Uncovering Biased Language

Assign students to find one or two articles in the library that contain examples of biased language. In class, have students rewrite the biased sections to eliminate the bias. If you can obtain a computer with a projection screen, you can actually rewrite the biased sections in front of the class to incorporate their suggestions.

One way to do this exercise is to have students find articles from the 1950s, 1960s, 1970s, 1980s, and 1990s from the same journal. Have them content-analyze the articles for biased language. Do they note any changes in how racial, religious, ethnic, or gender groups are referred to?

Building an APA-Style Paper

To illustrate how an APA-style paper should be written, you can use a class meeting to build a paper. Use one of the research projects conducted during the semester and have students contribute ideas about how each major section should be written. This exercise will work best if you can obtain a computer with a projection screen. Type in the suggestions, then edit the text for maximum clarity and completeness.

Using Internet Resources

A variety of sources of information on APA writing style is available on the Internet. For this exercise have students find some of the resources available on the Internet to help them write APA-style papers. Here are a few Web sites (valid at the time of this writing) that you can explore before doing the exercise. You can make these resources available to your students as part of this exercise.

<http://www.apa.org/students/faqsmenu.html>

This APA site has two sources concerning APA writing style. One answers frequently asked questions about APA style. For example, a resolution for conflicting information concerning the title page is provided. There is also a resource for how to cite information from the World Wide Web.

<http://www.wisc.edu/writetest/Handbook/main.html>

This is the University of Wisconsin at Madison Web site. The document available at this address provides a comprehensive handbook on writing. Students can find information on grammar and style and documentation styles. If you click on the "documentation styles" item on the menu you will be taken to another menu that includes APA style. Clicking on the APA menu item brings up a guide for doing APA-style citations.

<http://uwsp.edu/acad/psych/apa4b.htm>

At this University of Wisconsin–Stevens Point Web site you will find a comprehensive guide to writing research reports using APA style. The first page includes a detailed menu of a number of topics. Information can be found concerning general writing topics (typing, style details, numbers, citations) as well as information specific to each section of an APA paper. Overviews of the main points of APA style are provided along with manuscript-like examples.

<http://www.ldl.net/apatwo.htm>

This Web site provides yet another guide to writing in APA style. It is less comprehensive than the University of Wisconsin–Stevens Point offering. However, it does provide brief descriptions of APA style points and provides good examples of citation formats.

CHAPTER 14

USING MULTIVARIATE DESIGN AND ANALYSIS

KEY QUESTIONS TO CONSIDER

- What statistics are used to evaluate correlational and experimental multivariate relationships?
- What are the key assumptions and requirements of multivariate statistics?
- How do various violations of the assumptions underlying multivariate statistics affect your data analysis?
- When is factor analysis used?
- Why are factors rotated in factor analysis?
- What do partial and part correlations tell you?
- For what research applications would you use the various types of multiple regression?
- How are multiple R and the regression weights used to interpret the results from a multiple regression analysis?
- How is the squared semipartial correlation used to interpret the results from a regression analysis?
- When would you use a multivariate analysis of variance to analyze your data?
- How are the results from a multivariate analysis of variance interpreted?
- When is loglinear analysis used to analyze your data?
- What is path analysis and how is it used in the research process?

CHAPTER OUTLINE

Experimental and Correlational Multivariate Designs
    Correlational Multivariate Design
    Experimental Multivariate Design
        Multivariate Statistical Tests
        Advantages of the Experimental Multivariate Strategy
        Advantages of the Correlational Multivariate Strategy
    Causal Inference
Assumptions and Requirements of Multivariate Statistics
    Linearity
    Outliers
        Identifying Outliers
        Dealing With Outliers
    Normality and Homoscedasticity
    Multicollinearity
    Error of Measurement
    Sample Size
Multivariate Statistical Tests
    Factor Analysis
        Factor Loadings
        Rotation of Factors
        Principal Components and Principal Factors Analysis
        An Example of Factor Analysis
    Partial and Part Correlations

KEY TERMS

Univariate strategy	Partial correlation
Multivariate strategy	Part correlation
Multiple regression	Multiple R
Discriminant analysis	R-square
Canonical correlation	Beta weight
Factor analysis	Loglinear analysis
Multivariate analysis of variance (MANOVA)	Path analysis

CHAPTER GOALS

Chapter 14 provides an overview of multivariate statistical analysis. Our goal in writing this chapter was to introduce students to the major multivariate statistical procedures, including when they would be used, what they would be used for, and what the underlying logic is. Given the increasing use of multivariate statistical techniques, we feel that students should at least have some idea of what they are and why they are sometimes used in place of univariate statistics. It was not our intention to provide a thorough grounding in multivariate analysis.

In keeping with this goal, our coverage of multivariate techniques is broad rather than deep. The chapter begins by listing the most common correlational and experimental multivariate designs and explains the advantages of multivariate designs over univariate ones. This is followed by a discussion of the assumptions and requirements of multivariate statistics (linearity, outliers and how to deal with them, normality, homoscedasticity, multicollinearity, the issues of measurement error and sample size). The remainder of the chapter introduces specific multivariate techniques. For each technique, we indicate what the technique is used for, describe the major issues a researcher must deal with when using the technique, and provide an example of its use.

Key points to bring up in classroom discussions include:

- The requirements and assumptions of multivariate statistics. You should define each requirement/assumption and discuss how important it is that these be met.
- In factor analysis, the goal is to identify a small number of underlying variables (factors) that determine the scores on the measures given. The idea is that the scores obtained from each measure reflect the combined effects of two or more underlying variables. Factor analysis uses the pattern of intercorrelations between measures to "extract" the underlying factors.
- Part and partial correlations are attempts to statistically control the effects of extraneous "third" variables to determine how two variables would be related if the third variable were held constant. This offers a possible solution to the "third variable problem" that, along with the directionality problem, makes inferring cause from correlation dangerous.
- In multiple regression, multiple R can be interpreted simply as the ordinary Pearson correlation between the actual values of the criterion variable and the values predicted by the linear regression equation. You might want to explain how the order in which variables are entered into the analysis affects the weights assigned to the variables when the predictor variables are intercorrelated. Attempts to deal with this problem lead to the different types of regression analysis (simple, hierarchical, and stepwise).
- You might want to reinforce the main distinction between discriminant analysis and multiple regression, which is that discriminant analysis is used when the criterion variable is categorical (nominal scale), whereas multiple regression is used when the criterion variable falls on an interval or ratio scale.
- Canonical correlation is similar to multiple regression except that the criterion "variable" is a linear combination of variables similar to the linear combination of predictor variables.
- MANOVA is used when you have multiple dependent variables in a design that otherwise would call for ANOVA. The MANOVA helps to avoid the probability pyramiding that would occur if each dependent variable were tested separately. Moreover, it can identify combinations of dependent variables that may be sensitive to the manipulation of the independent variables when each dependent variable by itself is not sensitive enough to give significant results.
- Another important role for MANOVA is the analysis of data from within-subjects designs when you suspect that the homogeneity of covariance assumption required for a within-subjects ANOVA may be violated. Rather than assuming equal covariances, MANOVA takes the observed covariances into account when determining statistical significance.
- Loglinear analysis provides an alternative to traditional analyses in both correlational and experimental situations in which the dependent variables were categorical. It can also be used as a nonparametric alternative when the assumptions of parametric tests are suspected to have been violated.
- Path analysis is used to construct causal models. Describe how path analysis works. Perhaps have students evaluate an actual example of path analysis from the literature.

IDEAS FOR CLASS ACTIVITIES

One way to get students acquainted with multivariate data analysis is to describe a study that used a multivariate approach and then guide the students through the results of the statistical analysis. This can be particularly effective if your example comes from your own research and you can provide students with copies of the analysis as printed out by one of the major statistical packages such as SPSS-X. Avoid lengthy explanations of eigenvalues or Wilks's Lambda; instead, focus on the conclusions you were able to draw from the analysis.

Lens Model Study

This correlational study uses multiple correlation to determine the weighting a subject gives to various sources of information that are used to make a decision. According to the "lens model," a participant's judgment about something like the desirability of a particular political candidate depends upon many factors (termed "cues"), such as the candidate's party affiliation, position on the liberal–conservative scale, ability to communicate, religious views, and physical attractiveness. These characteristics are somehow combined to form the judgment.

If we assume that the participant is forming a judgment by, in effect, weighting each cue according to its importance and then adding the weighted cues, we can model the judgment using multiple regression. Multiple regression will find the set of weights that maximize the correlation between the actual judgments and the judgments predicted by the regression equation. The size of the multiple R, then, indicates the degree to which the participant's judgments can be predicted by a linear combination of the cues. Which cues affect the participant's judgments most strongly can be determined by analyzing the regression weights assigned to the cues.

Students usually enjoy this exercise even though they do not fully understand how multiple regression works. After all, it tells them something interesting about themselves!

The study involves having the class decide on something to make a judgment about and on the cues that will be given in order to form a decision. For example, they might want to determine how people judge the desirability of an automobile. The class might then debate which sources of information need to be included: styling, performance, fuel efficiency, color, interior roominess, and so forth. Eventually they should narrow the field of cues down to about five cues.

The next step is to create a measurement scale for each cue. These should be numerical rating scales with verbal anchors. For example, styling could be rated from 1 (ugly) to 7 (knockout). A similar scale needs to be created for the judgments, perhaps from 1 (you couldn't GIVE it to me) to 7 (I'd sell my soul for it). All the scales should be placed on a $3'' \times 5''$ card that the subject can refer to while making the judgments.

Now that the cue and judgment scales have been established, it is time to create a profile sheet. This sheet might look something like the following:

PROFILE NO. _____

    Styling   _____

    Performance   _____

    Fuel Efficiency   _____

    Safety Factor   _____

    Roominess   _____

Rating _____

Reproduce enough of the rating sheets to create 100 profiles for each member of the class. Number the profiles from 1 to 100 and fill in the cue values by random assignment. Leave the space labeled "Rating" blank.

Each student should be given a packet of 100 profiles. The students should be instructed to carefully examine each profile and try to imagine what the car (or whatever) being rated would be like based on the description provided by the ratings. The student should then fill in a rating for the profile based on this impression.

Analysis

Use a computerized statistical program to perform a multiple regression analysis of each student's ratings. This analysis should provide the multiple R, simple correlations between each pair of variables, standardized regression weights (beta weights), and, if possible, the squared semipartial correlations. Use the cue values as predictor variables and the ratings as the criterion variable. Obtain a printout of the analysis for each student and give it to the student.

The example given in the text to illustrate multiple correlation is in fact a study like the one described here. In that example we describe how to analyze and interpret the data, including how to calculate squared semipartial correlations, if need be. However, if the profiles have been constructed by choosing scale values at random, correlations between predictor variables will usually be low and in that case the beta weights themselves usually lead to conclusions similar to those based on the squared semipartial correlations. The variables given the largest weights will be those the student relied on most heavily to make a decision (assuming the linear model is valid). The size of R-square indicates the degree to which the linear model is able to predict the subject's judgments from the cue values.

CHAPTER 15

USING THEORY

KEY QUESTIONS TO CONSIDER

- What is a theory?
- How does a theory differ from a hypothesis, a model, and a law?
- What is a computer model and what are the advantages of constructing one?
- How do mechanistic and functional explanations differ? Which type of explanation is better, and why?
- How do quantitative, qualitative, analogical, and fundamental theories differ?
- What are the various roles that theories play in science?
- How do you know a good theory from a bad one?
- What are the major steps involved in developing a theory and what do you do at each step?
- What is meant by confirmation and disconfirmation of theories?
- How are theories effectively tested?
- What are the relative advantages and disadvantages of theory-driven and data-driven theories?

CHAPTER OUTLINE

What Is a Theory?
    Theory Versus Hypothesis
    Theory Versus Law
    Theory Versus Model
    Computer Modeling
    Mechanistic Versus Functional Explanations
Types of Theory
    Quantitative Versus Qualitative Theory
        Quantitative Theory
        Qualitative Theory
    Level of Description
        Descriptive Theories
        Analogical Theories
        Fundamental Theories
    Domain of a Theory
Roles of Theory in Science
    Understanding
    Prediction
    Organizing and Interpreting Research Results
    Generating Research
Characteristics of a Good Theory
    Ability to Account for Data
    Explanatory Relevance
    Testability
    Prediction of Novel Events
    Parsimony

KEY TERMS

Theory	Descriptive theory
Scientific theory	Analogical theory
Law	Fundamental theory
Model	Domain
Mechanistic explanation	Strong inference
Functional explanation	Confirmational strategy
Quantitative theory	Disconfirmational strategy
Qualitative theory	

CHAPTER GOALS

The research process begins with observation. The phenomena we observe often represent merely the surface manifestations of deeper processes, and to adequately explain those phenomena, we need to understand what those deeper processes are and how they interact. Such understanding is provided by theory. Chapter 15 discusses theory: the types of theory, what theories do (their role in science), how they are developed, what distinguishes a good theory from a bad one, how to test a theory, and the merits of theory-driven versus data-driven research. When they finish reading the chapter, students should have a strong grasp of how theory is used in science and why scientific theories are so important.

Points to emphasize in class include:

- The tentative nature of theories. Students should understand that even well-established theories can be overthrown if new evidence contradictory to the theory comes to light.
- The fact that theories can be proven false, but can never be proven true. We recently heard a "creation scientist" state that creation theory had been proven to be true. The statement said more about the speaker's understanding of science than it did about the theory. Students need to be shown why theories cannot be proven true and they need to understand why this does not weaken the force of scientific theories.
- The advantages of constructing computer models when developing and evaluating theory.
- The different types of theory and how to distinguish them. The explanations theories provide may be functional or mechanistic. Descriptive, analogical, and what we term "fundamental" theories represent different levels of understanding. Descriptive theories merely propose a relationship without really explaining

why the relationship exists; they are "surface" descriptions. Analogical theories attempt to relate the variables in the theory through analogy with known processes. Fundamental theories propose unobserved processes to explain the observed relationships. The processes themselves give rise to observable effects that, if they are in fact observed, provide indirect evidence for the existence of the proposed processes.

- The distinction between a qualitative theory and a quantitative one.
- What roles theories play in science.
- The steps to follow to develop a scientific theory.
- The difference between following a confirmational versus a disconfirmational strategy when testing a theory.
- The role theory plays in guiding scientific research.
- Why theories known to be inadequate often continue to be used (useful, no replacement in sight).
- The dangers of letting theory rather than data drive research, and vice versa. The advantage of combining the two approaches.

IDEAS FOR CLASS ACTIVITIES

Are Theories Necessary?

Have students read B. F. Skinner's article "Are Theories of Learning Necessary?" (the reference appears in the back of the text) and come to class prepared to debate the issue raised by the article. You can note the conditions that existed at the time the article was written (such as failure of Hullian theory to adequately account for all forms of learning) and use Skinner's argument to raise the question of when it is appropriate to attempt theory construction. Was Skinner too severe in his criticism? Is a science without theory really a science? What does Skinner propose to substitute in place of theory?

Strong Inference

Discuss Platt's suggestion that all we need to make progress in any science is to follow his program of "strong inference," or systematic elimination of rival hypotheses until only one (presumably the correct one) is left. What happens to strong inference when extraneous variables cannot be as rigorously controlled as they are in molecular biology? Is the apparent lack of progress in theoretical development within many fields of psychology due to a failure to follow Platt's methods, or might the complexity of relationships and lack of adequate control over the relevant variables have more to do with it?

Platt suggests that we attempt to develop several theories to account for our data and then rigorously pit the alternative theories against one another. Discuss the advantage of this approach over simply developing a theory and then testing its predictions.

The "competing theories" approach can be found in many studies on the "Observing Response" in the operant conditioning literature. An excellent example is

Wilton, R. N., & Clements, R. O. (1971). The role of information in the emission of observing responses: A test of two hypotheses. *Journal of the Experimental Analysis of Behavior, 16,* 161–166.

Paradigm Shift?

Kuhn (1964) suggested that scientists conduct their research under a set of implicit assumptions that constitute in effect a theory of the phenomena they study. This theory determines which research questions are important. When the theory is overthrown by a new view, a paradigm shift is said to occur. Under the new paradigm, new research questions become important and many issues that were important under the old view become irrelevant.

Many researchers now claim that American psychology is currently undergoing such a paradigm shift, from the purely associationistic view that predominated under behaviorism to a view that emphasizes mental processes. Discuss this "cognitive revolution" with the class. Does it represent a true paradigm shift as Kuhn would define one? In what ways does the cognitive view change one's approach to conducting research?

CHAPTER 16

MAKING SENSE OF RESEARCH

KEY QUESTIONS TO CONSIDER

- What are the criteria for acceptance of a manuscript?
- How does peer review work and what are some of the problems associated with it?
- How do you play the "publication game"?
- What are research fads and why do they emerge and die?
- What makes certain research areas more popular than others?
- What constitutes fraud in research and how prevalent is it?
- Why do scientists sometimes engage in fraudulent research practices?
- What steps can be taken to reduce the problem of fraud in research?
- How do values enter into the scientific process?
- How can scientists guard against values entering into their research?
- What is meta-analysis and how does it differ from a traditional literature review?
- What are the steps involved in conducting a meta-analysis?
- What are some of the problems associated with meta-analysis, and how can they be dealt with?

CHAPTER OUTLINE

Publication Practices
    Criteria for Acceptance of a Manuscript
        Statistical Significance
        Consistency With Previous Knowledge
        Significance of the Contribution
        Editorial Policy
    Pernicious Problems of Peer Review
        Peer Review
        Problems With Peer Review
    Playing the Publication Game
Fads in Research
    Fads Versus Trends in Research
    Why Fads Emerge and Die
    Reasons for Increased Popularity of a Research Area
        Research Interests Fit the "Spirit of the Times"
        A Particular Theory Appears to Have Great Theoretical Power
        Appropriate Research Instruments and Methodology Are Already Available
        Prestigious, Widely Respected Researchers Are Working in the Area
        There Is Strong Financial Support for Research Grants in the Area
        An Area Is on the Frontier of Unexplored Scientific Territory
    Reasons for Decreased Popularity of a Research Area
        Feelings That the Important Aspects of the Problem Are Already Solved
        Research Appears to Lead to an Empirical Dead End
        Research in the Area Is Shown to Be Flawed by Artifacts and Poor Methodology

KEY TERMS

File drawer phenomenon
Paradigm
Normal science
Paradigm shift
Peer review

Research fad
Research trend
Traditional literature review
Meta-analysis

CHAPTER GOALS

Chapter 16 contains three separate sections, the first addressing the impact of publication practices on the content of the scientific literature and an author's strategy for getting a manuscript published, the second discussing fraud and the role of values in science, and the third addressing how to integrate the results of studies within a field despite differences in methodology, variables manipulated and controlled, and results obtained. Students should come away from this chapter with a better appreciation of what a researcher is up against when trying to get a study published: how the theoretical biases of the reviewers, insistence on a finding of statistical significance, and unreliability of the review process contribute to the acceptance or rejection of a paper and ultimately color the conclusions one can draw from the published literature. They should also know some general rules to follow in order to maximize the chances of acceptance of their own papers.

The section on fraud and the role of values in science illustrates how science and scientists are often looked upon in unrealistic ways, with only the advancement of science and the best interests of humankind as goals. The section on fraud and values shows students that scientists, in the case of fraud, are sometimes motivated by the desire for prestige, power, or money. Students should also come away with the notion that a scientist's values may permeate his or her research, influencing the methods chosen, the manner in which data are collected, and how results are analyzed and interpreted.

Finally, students should be familiar with strategies for reviewing the literature, including the traditional literature review and the meta-analysis. Points to emphasize in class include

- How manuscripts submitted for publication are reviewed.
- What criteria are used to evaluate a manuscript.
- What peer review is and whether it seems to be working as well as it should.
- What factors contribute to the rejection of a manuscript (e.g., the study's conclusions at variance with the reviewer's beliefs).
- The reliability (or unreliability) of peer review.
- What to do when your manuscript is rejected.
- The distinction between research fads and research trends, and what factors contribute to their emergence and disappearance.
- How and why research fraud is committed and what can be done about it.
- How a scientist's values might influence how research is done and how research results are interpreted.
- What the "file drawer phenomenon" is, how it relates to the use of statistical significance testing, and how it may affect the actual Type I error rate in published studies.
- The steps to follow when conducting a meta-analysis.
- The strengths and weaknesses of meta-analysis.

IDEAS FOR CLASS ACTIVITIES

Mock Review

If your students have created research papers based on their laboratory research, you can use these as the candidate manuscripts for a literature review. Divide the class into several "editorial boards" of about three students each. Each editorial board should then elect an "editor" who will take charge of the review process. Collect the research papers and distribute them to the editorial boards, making sure that no board receives papers from its own members. The editor should receive the papers, mark the cover and abstract pages with an identifying number, and remove and save the cover page so that the identity of the author will not be known to the reviewers. The editor should then give the paper to one of the reviewers.

Because the number of papers will equal the number of students, each board should receive one paper for each board member. Initially, then, the reviewers and the editor will receive one paper each to review. They should read this paper (between class meetings), make their comments and recommendations on paper, and then exchange papers, until each member has reviewed all the papers.

The editor should then collect all the reviewers' comments for a given paper and, based on these, should decide whether to accept or reject the paper. At the next class meeting, the editors should return the manuscripts (cover pages attached) to their authors, together with a note indicating whether the paper was accepted or rejected and the reviewers' comments.

You can then have the class discuss the exercise and the insights they have gained about the review process. For example, you might have each editorial group discuss the problems they encountered with the manuscripts (in general terms) and in reaching a decision.

Uncovering Fraud in Research

Chapter 16 discusses the problem of fraud in research. Have students find a case of research fraud and analyze why the fraud took place using the material in the chapter. Students could also, based on the motives of the scientists who committed the fraud, suggest how the fraud could have been prevented and how similar fraud could be prevented in the future. Case studies can be found in the following sources:

Bell, R. (1992). *Impure science.* New York: John Wiley & Sons.

Joynson, R. B. (1989). *The Burt affair.* London: Routledge.

Exploring Values in Research

Have students go to the library, perhaps in teams, and find articles in which the authors have allowed their own values to permeate their work. You might suggest that students focus their search on issues that have some political or cultural implications (e.g., gender differences, gender roles, research on gun control, research on family disintegration). You could have the students identify specific ways in which they feel that the methods chosen and interpretation of data were influenced by the author's values or attitudes.

Resource

Longino, H. E. (1990). *Science as social knowledge: Values and objectivity in scientific inquiry.* Princeton, NJ: Princeton University Press.

Exploring a Meta-Analysis

Find a recent literature review that included a meta-analysis of the findings and distribute copies to the class. Go over the paper with them and point out how meta-analysis was used to support the conclusions drawn by the authors. Note which meta-analytic techniques were used in the paper, and compare this approach to the traditional literature review that does not include a meta-analysis.

APPENDIX I

CODING SHEET FOR PRIMATE OBSERVATIONAL STUDY

Name:_____

Primate Behavior Checksheet

Date:_____ Time:_____ Weather:_____
Species:_____ Individual:_____

	BEHAVIORS Check behavior once per interval if it occurs			ACTIVITY LEVEL Rate at the beep				COMMENTS
				1	2	3	4	
1								
2								
3								
4								
5								
6								
7								
8								
9								
10								
11								
12								
13								
14								
15								
16								
17								
18								
19								
20								
21								
22								
23								
24								
25								
26								
27								
28								
29								
30								
TOTALS								
PERCENTAGES								

APPENDIX II

POPULATION VALUES RANGING FROM ONE TO FIFTY

Population of 1000 values ranging from 1 to 25

	1	2	3	4	5	6	7	8	9	10	11	12	13	14	15	16	17	18	19	20
1	14	8	19	25	11	11	19	21	4	17	13	18	2	5	16	18	17	16	20	3
2	13	13	17	14	7	7	21	19	2	13	11	17	3	15	25	7	22	1	23	12
3	1	25	10	25	13	16	24	25	3	15	17	13	24	20	25	12	21	14	7	10
4	18	3	4	5	8	19	21	17	8	16	18	1	1	7	24	21	4	2	17	6
5	20	23	13	11	16	10	22	14	3	2	21	8	15	3	10	19	13	10	19	3
6	1	23	25	25	22	13	6	17	7	6	8	15	5	1	4	21	4	23	25	6
7	15	13	18	21	2	20	5	4	17	6	14	4	13	20	19	10	6	12	2	5
8	20	11	3	25	3	16	21	8	11	22	25	12	16	6	21	8	6	23	7	3
9	3	9	12	22	11	1	23	15	18	20	4	3	11	9	17	10	23	16	6	2
10	11	22	18	14	17	12	4	11	22	19	20	4	15	1	23	4	18	13	14	7
11	25	19	24	9	15	8	8	13	8	6	3	25	11	14	25	4	24	5	6	21
12	11	3	16	20	10	24	19	10	12	1	22	15	14	11	22	24	8	3	22	2
13	15	24	21	15	22	11	20	10	20	3	16	12	4	6	5	11	5	23	3	18
14	23	13	1	3	22	18	1	3	10	2	20	15	9	12	21	2	10	6	2	17
15	10	18	17	6	22	25	11	6	3	1	11	20	16	21	10	18	12	6	10	3
16	8	25	3	13	19	20	3	4	22	15	1	23	24	6	13	9	6	18	22	11
17	20	17	14	1	8	22	8	17	17	9	21	11	7	6	11	6	9	6	19	8
18	9	3	18	9	15	19	3	2	12	6	18	25	7	14	15	11	21	14	8	19
19	23	6	24	18	6	17	22	23	6	7	10	17	3	12	13	16	9	25	7	21
20	16	24	16	22	2	13	24	16	9	21	21	1	11	20	6	16	18	17	5	19
21	22	19	22	21	15	11	16	19	9	14	17	6	10	18	22	23	4	20	12	24
22	3	17	15	23	13	17	25	4	1	2	19	17	4	18	10	7	12	16	14	5
23	13	19	19	22	5	23	10	20	23	20	7	7	18	24	6	9	10	11	9	6
24	5	9	12	17	12	12	12	23	15	21	19	18	20	16	20	18	3	13	14	3
25	5	6	19	4	20	19	14	14	5	5	7	2	24	11	19	12	19	16	24	10
26	2	19	21	13	2	1	24	17	24	23	11	9	10	4	18	22	9	1	10	4
27	2	25	14	25	17	17	19	20	5	3	1	2	4	3	9	6	6	17	4	23
28	6	2	15	23	5	18	5	6	13	19	18	7	3	13	19	10	12	3	2	5
29	15	24	6	20	8	19	2	22	2	20	4	17	5	11	6	1	23	12	17	19
30	14	1	12	7	9	9	10	23	5	4	23	4	5	15	9	4	7	11	21	18
31	8	17	16	10	18	24	3	24	5	5	23	13	1	21	21	24	18	19	18	7
32	9	21	2	1	14	17	15	8	22	24	12	16	18	3	24	16	12	5	15	16
33	3	23	23	9	17	7	22	16	5	18	20	8	5	16	24	1	22	4	11	4
34	6	3	24	18	22	22	10	1	19	2	13	1	9	24	5	16	11	10	23	20
35	16	3	14	1	15	14	12	9	17	4	17	4	15	19	7	13	12	9	3	11
36	15	5	11	1	22	22	10	10	12	8	7	13	22	13	20	17	5	3	5	25
37	25	5	12	12	13	18	16	25	25	19	23	22	18	13	10	8	6	12	15	10
38	3	2	8	3	19	6	2	11	10	11	5	21	7	25	9	20	17	22	4	12
39	1	2	16	9	15	17	1	13	8	24	6	24	23	22	14	11	24	9	20	20
40	4	25	5	19	11	12	2	14	24	3	3	17	1	1	21	6	8	18	16	3
41	15	15	25	1	15	20	13	15	6	21	5	7	6	23	12	11	22	24	20	21
42	12	7	22	18	10	5	23	21	20	5	23	13	21	2	23	5	4	25	21	4
43	6	6	9	17	2	19	20	12	11	24	24	8	13	9	22	2	14	19	2	19
44	13	6	8	1	10	7	11	20	19	17	6	2	13	25	5	19	22	17	16	7
45	9	5	9	7	16	6	15	16	20	19	10	15	18	11	19	21	1	9	4	17
46	18	1	14	17	18	7	10	15	11	6	1	8	10	19	3	18	13	21	15	18
47	11	2	19	5	10	24	21	24	23	19	5	9	16	5	15	17	7	1	13	7
48	8	16	12	20	18	25	18	6	1	4	15	25	18	5	23	14	5	11	16	9
49	19	5	23	1	6	11	9	6	17	23	24	2	19	13	5	22	1	10	22	2
50	10	4	7	13	20	13	9	18	12	1	21	23	17	16	24	15	14	24	21	21

Population of 1000 values ranging from 6 to 30

	1	2	3	4	5	6	7	8	9	10	11	12	13	14	15	16	17	18	19	20
1	8	12	20	30	10	24	10	12	10	22	7	29	23	15	30	12	8	7	12	17
2	26	10	28	25	23	17	11	18	26	30	21	16	7	17	29	13	11	18	23	9
3	29	24	11	20	18	23	6	20	29	23	26	7	12	7	29	26	30	10	15	11
4	27	9	9	7	16	21	27	21	23	25	19	30	18	16	22	6	6	15	14	8
5	10	8	30	28	8	9	20	29	12	8	23	14	6	28	10	7	7	7	7	14
6	20	7	6	20	16	24	15	18	8	19	24	29	16	13	29	15	7	25	26	10
7	15	29	25	27	6	25	27	15	20	25	14	7	30	28	25	15	22	21	27	27
8	18	9	12	8	23	24	6	7	18	23	25	18	8	10	12	27	18	6	13	29
9	11	12	11	18	25	6	22	19	13	12	27	15	24	25	27	17	24	13	21	30
10	9	27	14	8	10	9	12	20	23	6	14	13	9	22	14	30	6	24	16	12
11	29	22	28	12	23	15	20	27	23	23	24	24	13	14	12	22	11	27	24	17
12	23	26	6	30	27	28	11	7	14	13	12	18	27	9	16	19	15	10	12	7
13	6	23	7	9	22	23	29	28	14	16	6	18	10	10	6	28	14	9	6	30
14	26	8	10	21	14	11	15	25	11	19	20	17	13	28	18	17	13	19	17	9
15	19	9	9	23	27	17	19	11	30	18	15	12	14	26	22	11	8	25	22	13
16	9	28	16	14	16	22	16	19	11	29	9	22	28	17	16	28	20	9	24	18
17	21	22	13	27	25	24	8	26	23	10	9	30	13	15	10	6	7	21	17	18
18	24	20	14	17	11	8	12	28	25	7	28	18	25	30	16	11	12	13	14	19
19	8	11	6	13	21	6	17	26	29	28	18	25	21	22	30	16	12	15	19	22
20	11	21	28	27	12	6	26	9	10	23	17	14	14	20	18	15	25	30	15	10
21	12	11	21	7	22	28	21	27	18	24	20	17	13	22	24	22	12	26	22	24
22	12	12	20	7	30	19	11	14	30	26	21	30	7	25	14	12	13	8	11	8
23	23	11	28	19	19	15	19	11	27	11	8	26	6	23	17	27	18	23	6	24
24	16	15	29	10	28	25	17	27	21	12	22	27	25	21	20	8	19	26	15	27
25	9	10	15	7	18	15	7	30	15	10	7	20	21	14	27	20	23	7	21	15
26	10	19	28	17	25	9	9	19	18	29	19	13	9	21	20	11	7	14	24	15
27	12	23	24	13	16	22	25	6	15	10	11	14	29	25	10	18	22	29	27	22
28	7	21	10	24	25	25	9	25	17	28	25	26	21	30	16	17	6	17	8	30
29	18	10	30	16	12	9	28	21	18	12	9	25	18	13	10	23	16	8	10	16
30	18	10	21	26	16	8	9	20	19	27	22	18	24	11	25	18	29	21	20	16
31	9	9	30	8	22	15	9	9	21	26	28	24	12	25	27	23	26	17	19	6
32	20	28	12	9	30	15	11	28	7	15	21	29	9	22	9	13	21	12	8	26
33	29	27	13	14	27	21	7	19	19	8	26	29	24	25	30	15	7	12	8	16
34	30	16	25	6	23	23	7	27	6	14	12	16	18	7	30	8	22	7	9	26
35	10	18	22	19	19	27	15	10	22	15	11	12	12	13	10	20	9	27	6	21
36	8	21	8	26	27	22	21	30	30	20	10	15	12	30	29	28	24	15	18	14
37	10	20	9	26	19	17	15	21	24	14	12	18	29	30	6	9	21	30	11	20
38	13	21	17	15	15	7	27	18	20	27	22	11	26	10	7	14	10	16	29	10
39	23	24	28	6	17	24	17	9	27	17	26	15	10	19	19	17	7	24	21	11
40	15	12	13	23	28	8	24	7	18	21	6	23	10	19	15	19	17	24	24	22
41	10	23	24	13	15	18	26	25	28	19	18	20	9	28	27	22	6	22	14	26
42	16	19	22	22	22	10	14	23	28	28	13	16	18	15	22	25	14	15	29	17
43	30	23	21	26	14	7	8	17	26	17	6	30	15	10	19	12	24	9	13	13
44	23	7	24	14	11	7	30	25	28	23	18	25	22	25	14	16	27	13	15	28
45	15	30	26	10	20	29	20	28	21	30	8	18	10	28	15	30	29	19	16	12
46	26	29	23	20	6	29	26	26	19	12	25	7	11	21	23	29	16	24	28	21
47	7	27	15	23	14	24	22	21	16	13	6	12	7	17	13	27	8	11	15	20
48	17	15	17	18	9	9	7	26	26	17	20	11	18	30	23	8	18	15	18	7
49	18	14	30	29	17	20	12	6	27	17	27	18	26	20	6	6	23	18	13	27
50	18	27	15	18	8	7	13	6	6	12	16	15	13	10	18	21	26	14	7	24

Population of 1000 values ranging from 11 to 35

	1	2	3	4	5	6	7	8	9	10	11	12	13	14	15	16	17	18	19	20
1	18	27	19	32	13	21	16	23	21	20	18	25	28	35	27	19	31	20	29	31
2	16	31	26	31	34	13	34	11	14	18	15	21	25	26	13	11	26	19	23	17
3	11	22	11	32	17	21	23	35	22	25	29	14	26	23	16	28	22	32	11	16
4	14	16	16	19	32	28	19	11	13	17	13	19	17	13	30	24	13	18	20	35
5	28	19	22	12	34	30	12	32	17	11	17	28	34	22	34	14	23	18	32	26
6	30	31	13	27	29	35	35	21	21	21	21	32	25	21	34	30	19	24	35	31
7	27	13	16	27	20	26	28	26	21	13	11	30	20	15	14	12	11	13	18	31
8	19	14	26	34	24	11	32	28	23	31	21	26	20	30	33	27	27	30	22	18
9	19	35	16	18	28	27	18	35	24	16	19	12	27	12	24	20	15	16	13	22
10	28	30	29	24	22	11	27	15	26	12	28	34	20	20	21	16	28	25	22	22
11	14	20	25	23	21	29	33	23	19	35	27	30	20	27	22	17	29	14	35	17
12	14	35	21	26	30	26	23	11	28	35	33	19	16	27	14	14	23	31	18	23
13	26	33	12	28	11	23	24	34	16	35	27	26	31	30	24	31	22	24	12	13
14	29	28	12	35	20	31	24	31	15	22	23	16	12	33	22	32	23	23	25	20
15	20	22	22	28	18	25	29	24	13	32	30	31	29	28	24	11	33	32	13	23
16	26	28	26	12	21	21	22	27	28	29	17	22	20	22	16	15	19	14	19	15
17	25	28	32	25	15	23	31	25	30	27	31	30	14	25	21	24	12	34	16	20
18	20	30	31	18	17	35	24	21	23	28	17	11	21	26	28	34	29	22	33	24
19	12	11	16	17	33	24	13	35	14	26	25	24	18	13	26	22	34	12	16	28
20	25	27	22	17	25	23	26	20	35	15	18	31	18	20	26	33	27	16	24	26
21	25	23	26	15	13	35	20	34	24	34	19	17	26	27	27	19	30	35	34	22
22	35	12	20	20	21	14	31	18	14	11	28	29	26	35	30	22	22	24	26	31
23	33	16	13	28	24	29	23	21	21	25	30	28	20	20	24	14	20	15	21	19
24	31	27	19	18	21	11	28	31	16	18	33	35	27	15	19	18	21	18	13	11
25	25	27	25	15	22	17	16	20	33	22	17	25	29	22	35	22	19	24	17	34
26	25	15	33	21	29	21	31	14	35	35	14	25	35	28	15	16	35	29	12	27
27	28	21	22	25	19	17	31	35	31	26	19	34	22	35	21	28	33	15	11	20
28	11	23	13	32	33	22	23	17	14	22	26	34	30	23	31	13	14	32	35	23
29	31	23	24	25	32	25	27	34	32	21	24	33	11	35	15	27	24	31	15	30
30	22	27	26	12	28	12	32	15	24	13	27	23	26	21	11	18	15	19	22	24
31	29	11	23	21	26	17	33	14	19	18	29	21	29	11	27	20	29	23	35	24
32	11	25	17	25	35	28	17	33	31	14	32	13	19	11	19	31	13	17	19	26
33	24	12	13	19	26	24	21	19	35	18	34	28	18	22	18	13	35	15	16	24
34	33	35	15	21	28	27	15	25	33	12	30	26	19	28	19	19	18	29	12	14
35	22	14	19	23	16	17	12	20	33	12	14	15	20	35	13	16	22	26	35	28
36	35	34	20	21	18	11	29	31	12	25	14	15	33	16	15	32	19	28	13	31
37	33	27	21	23	22	32	33	32	34	21	33	19	21	19	11	21	28	15	24	26
38	32	13	32	28	18	16	32	35	24	33	23	31	33	11	17	11	23	28	23	25
39	31	29	34	12	25	19	18	31	11	24	30	33	16	28	23	12	35	29	21	15
40	16	27	31	30	25	19	28	28	24	26	33	19	35	11	13	20	17	30	13	13
41	33	11	29	34	29	12	12	16	29	22	16	15	33	18	12	35	31	20	16	14
42	16	19	17	35	32	26	12	16	33	11	16	19	30	32	26	11	30	21	15	18
43	30	13	16	32	13	17	31	31	31	21	34	23	17	31	12	15	23	25	15	20
44	18	23	32	33	28	19	18	22	26	12	21	11	33	21	30	25	12	12	33	13
45	30	22	11	17	26	30	27	21	11	17	35	34	22	11	27	19	31	13	21	12
46	23	34	28	34	34	19	33	33	12	34	29	16	22	19	11	34	12	27	27	35
47	24	23	18	20	12	14	19	11	35	13	16	22	19	33	22	26	26	12	20	24
48	16	33	20	24	19	31	23	33	28	16	21	27	31	20	30	21	28	23	26	30
49	12	28	14	33	35	31	16	32	32	19	33	33	28	20	14	14	31	30	33	27
50	11	16	11	35	26	34	24	35	12	28	16	26	21	27	13	18	35	19	22	31

Population of 1000 values ranging from 16 to 40

	1	2	3	4	5	6	7	8	9	10	11	12	13	14	15	16	17	18	19	20
1	20	36	34	17	27	31	34	21	40	25	34	27	29	37	26	38	20	37	20	19
2	19	22	16	38	16	22	34	39	29	18	23	37	36	35	25	28	39	18	34	38
3	19	34	22	35	20	34	29	30	20	31	16	39	20	38	23	35	17	18	26	28
4	29	27	31	37	33	21	40	40	39	40	38	33	34	38	38	20	16	22	25	25
5	38	18	32	37	25	39	24	37	40	38	30	37	31	17	39	21	39	34	16	27
6	26	27	23	39	17	28	33	37	36	30	37	38	19	38	29	28	37	33	38	21
7	39	40	29	28	40	35	34	39	40	24	28	26	18	26	39	25	20	39	22	36
8	22	37	16	34	21	16	34	20	40	36	16	28	32	35	17	30	27	38	36	21
9	39	16	27	28	20	30	20	17	27	38	37	26	31	16	31	19	30	19	28	35
10	22	22	17	32	18	33	37	40	19	21	27	17	24	19	32	40	28	27	29	32
11	30	24	40	34	17	40	17	25	40	40	23	36	24	35	28	40	19	21	21	34
12	21	20	21	29	30	35	19	37	39	32	16	32	31	37	21	33	36	17	35	17
13	31	35	25	25	38	21	40	35	24	25	29	20	34	31	35	20	30	23	26	34
14	34	28	35	34	16	34	35	30	37	28	21	29	34	37	17	27	39	26	33	33
15	29	32	29	20	34	22	39	38	20	28	26	23	26	34	25	17	38	35	37	26
16	16	21	20	28	27	18	22	36	39	34	38	28	27	29	26	30	39	16	21	30
17	37	21	40	29	19	34	32	25	38	26	18	29	37	39	33	29	39	31	24	21
18	24	18	36	24	32	39	19	34	26	34	26	31	38	38	36	20	23	32	19	23
19	34	38	20	36	25	33	17	30	35	35	29	27	32	21	19	19	39	31	39	33
20	33	36	19	24	39	34	22	30	26	27	29	36	32	22	29	32	21	37	33	34
21	28	26	34	32	40	26	39	21	38	25	17	16	40	19	24	21	23	29	36	17
22	28	31	34	31	18	25	36	18	16	29	21	37	31	23	18	26	21	37	40	19
23	32	34	28	16	26	39	25	33	19	31	30	18	30	17	19	27	22	37	40	23
24	30	24	20	27	32	37	19	27	29	23	32	31	30	33	23	35	30	28	25	32
25	27	24	25	27	19	31	17	28	22	22	19	29	20	31	39	35	35	35	38	39
26	33	25	18	34	17	25	28	25	16	36	31	39	17	35	37	21	28	29	31	31
27	24	24	38	20	37	16	38	40	28	30	18	31	32	17	33	21	25	27	26	24
28	33	34	24	29	28	32	20	30	19	22	40	16	33	40	36	34	21	26	23	24
29	17	19	26	32	22	37	23	34	29	21	25	25	24	38	33	30	40	33	30	20
30	22	34	23	27	36	30	27	36	35	31	22	16	38	28	22	16	38	25	36	18
31	20	38	28	40	26	23	28	29	34	27	19	33	38	28	28	21	35	21	29	31
32	39	31	35	25	24	19	39	37	19	32	39	19	17	33	31	31	29	16	38	38
33	20	28	40	21	31	18	22	34	20	25	39	35	17	31	17	25	33	40	23	26
34	38	39	35	19	23	20	17	38	18	39	35	34	16	37	39	18	27	19	36	40
35	37	28	23	37	23	39	40	16	22	19	26	39	26	27	31	19	38	22	31	35
36	19	22	26	34	34	27	23	36	21	16	21	30	31	34	34	30	17	25	38	27
37	18	34	27	31	24	33	33	40	29	24	40	16	17	25	37	30	27	40	19	38
38	38	27	37	40	26	22	19	34	19	34	30	20	38	19	35	21	29	39	32	24
39	33	22	20	21	36	16	26	39	38	40	27	28	29	24	20	18	32	33	39	23
40	38	31	38	23	38	18	37	22	32	30	17	33	28	32	28	18	40	33	32	24
41	25	20	24	16	26	17	20	40	35	18	37	23	19	25	36	29	40	16	31	26
42	26	38	29	38	25	35	22	25	33	32	30	24	36	38	18	27	23	39	18	33
43	21	16	32	18	20	36	31	25	30	30	35	25	23	34	32	25	24	21	23	30
44	30	31	40	27	40	32	23	33	37	25	21	16	40	34	29	35	38	28	20	20
45	34	32	38	29	38	26	22	22	19	36	34	20	36	23	27	35	33	32	33	34
46	23	29	27	21	36	32	21	35	24	40	36	17	19	30	38	31	25	32	24	31
47	36	18	24	23	27	28	31	29	27	20	40	31	24	24	32	21	39	38	19	37
48	34	16	25	20	29	18	24	22	40	20	34	34	18	35	20	35	17	22	33	32
49	30	31	17	29	32	33	39	31	37	22	23	29	19	38	16	40	19	28	16	37
50	40	37	39	20	21	40	26	16	31	34	22	29	19	29	36	27	20	31	27	16

Population of 1000 values ranging from 21 to 45

	1	2	3	4	5	6	7	8	9	10	11	12	13	14	15	16	17	18	19	20
1	24	22	35	38	30	38	24	35	24	39	26	45	43	44	34	23	39	21	39	35
2	27	33	29	31	38	40	34	37	30	40	26	25	25	22	36	45	44	36	34	21
3	25	42	33	36	26	45	21	44	44	38	27	21	31	27	24	45	27	34	36	23
4	37	28	36	35	34	34	40	39	28	33	34	44	30	35	36	25	39	27	23	37
5	36	39	25	42	26	40	25	26	31	39	44	27	34	42	26	39	34	40	30	21
6	21	35	21	34	29	31	24	38	38	23	26	45	28	39	35	42	21	32	44	25
7	43	43	22	31	41	23	22	43	28	28	34	37	31	31	34	33	35	33	36	34
8	26	41	28	23	21	34	33	30	23	36	35	30	30	26	31	40	35	33	26	43
9	43	41	43	44	23	42	23	27	29	29	33	27	45	44	42	29	27	34	44	41
10	35	35	34	31	28	43	32	41	39	29	36	33	44	36	36	24	43	26	43	21
11	42	26	29	34	26	21	23	34	43	26	44	42	28	30	42	22	23	25	38	25
12	43	39	36	27	37	25	35	29	41	22	44	34	22	37	34	39	26	35	39	37
13	45	22	37	26	41	27	33	41	36	34	35	37	29	44	23	23	43	39	32	26
14	38	35	35	38	26	37	26	36	40	45	31	23	45	32	31	40	33	26	33	25
15	45	23	43	22	30	29	26	29	35	28	40	24	38	32	33	39	35	26	45	30
16	34	26	28	26	28	27	42	39	26	34	45	37	38	28	35	26	29	38	24	38
17	25	36	29	36	30	24	26	32	35	38	36	37	28	43	40	43	42	43	36	25
18	31	21	39	41	34	31	35	21	29	34	24	30	35	30	26	28	42	29	21	29
19	26	24	29	45	25	25	45	31	44	21	28	42	24	25	21	31	39	40	36	35
20	29	30	42	29	31	38	42	24	22	34	30	43	21	38	35	30	33	35	31	21
21	25	45	35	29	31	24	27	21	36	42	23	22	37	26	26	40	25	33	39	45
22	26	38	30	35	23	35	43	27	35	45	41	25	41	40	26	40	22	41	31	33
23	40	39	38	27	31	42	41	32	45	37	41	26	25	40	41	45	40	25	28	39
24	45	37	32	43	24	31	34	38	36	41	21	32	42	21	38	22	34	29	37	35
25	33	28	29	23	36	22	29	40	22	44	43	32	28	45	25	38	22	41	31	36
26	28	45	24	23	24	29	23	33	27	28	45	31	22	31	36	23	38	34	34	43
27	36	21	38	23	25	29	38	40	45	29	34	40	38	41	22	45	44	21	27	23
28	45	28	39	31	43	24	42	35	28	30	23	40	35	32	30	26	34	26	29	42
29	32	27	37	21	27	36	37	38	24	33	26	38	21	21	37	21	24	36	44	21
30	23	30	43	23	27	37	29	34	43	39	37	36	23	29	21	24	26	30	23	31
31	31	42	27	30	36	23	38	31	22	42	39	24	41	43	34	25	32	27	31	26
32	33	25	25	24	23	38	24	29	22	25	31	22	45	28	30	36	43	44	27	41
33	37	34	41	45	23	44	21	42	42	23	37	40	21	23	33	45	30	29	34	22
34	45	24	27	21	33	34	38	43	31	21	23	35	26	34	42	28	40	26	44	23
35	25	30	21	43	44	41	30	31	45	43	21	31	35	25	40	30	24	40	31	30
36	29	40	44	21	24	23	30	36	42	29	27	29	21	27	38	44	42	32	45	27
37	25	43	34	43	26	38	43	31	45	40	41	39	38	29	28	40	44	29	34	44
38	27	26	31	38	35	28	32	35	42	42	34	45	24	37	31	28	21	29	42	32
39	28	39	40	28	40	25	44	24	38	31	30	45	34	26	31	31	28	44	42	41
40	39	41	31	28	44	40	41	28	25	36	25	34	27	34	36	43	35	34	32	40
41	34	27	25	35	38	44	39	29	39	26	31	38	31	42	30	43	42	38	31	29
42	30	23	33	33	21	37	23	40	42	35	30	35	40	22	29	25	45	32	27	45
43	38	31	43	40	27	28	21	42	40	27	34	26	40	34	37	27	27	30	36	37
44	34	37	32	22	27	45	31	38	34	23	22	21	40	25	41	24	29	36	21	43
45	44	41	24	33	22	29	36	41	28	25	43	44	35	24	26	34	25	29	34	44
46	40	38	21	40	24	31	26	24	44	36	29	26	23	45	42	29	44	41	24	43
47	21	30	45	42	28	22	31	41	30	26	26	32	27	28	25	41	27	34	33	27
48	45	30	26	32	32	41	38	38	36	27	41	38	41	25	40	25	26	36	22	41
49	21	42	26	32	30	41	29	26	41	35	24	40	24	36	27	31	43	24	26	32
50	32	41	29	36	25	40	39	33	37	39	34	45	36	40	25	25	25	45	23	37

Population of 1000 values ranging from 26 to 50

	1	2	3	4	5	6	7	8	9	10	11	12	13	14	15	16	17	18	19	20
1	44	32	48	48	36	48	45	48	30	31	29	30	46	32	35	28	33	29	38	49
2	34	45	41	42	46	48	41	33	28	28	45	34	40	46	43	30	41	28	37	27
3	28	30	32	41	35	43	30	30	31	35	27	47	41	48	26	29	43	26	30	44
4	41	50	48	28	29	48	45	40	30	26	47	40	28	31	43	34	31	41	29	47
5	37	38	28	26	34	35	45	43	31	46	40	50	34	50	26	37	39	32	32	48
6	39	26	43	34	40	38	48	35	47	31	27	35	33	46	42	47	47	29	35	49
7	37	27	43	33	41	31	34	39	34	36	43	26	26	39	30	39	37	37	36	49
8	49	31	34	38	29	39	40	26	40	30	29	50	42	42	48	44	40	27	35	37
9	28	33	42	28	36	44	31	35	46	28	42	40	44	29	28	48	27	43	31	32
10	33	31	32	50	42	36	40	47	38	49	45	49	43	26	45	36	34	31	47	27
11	39	39	49	28	31	49	50	43	43	43	42	39	48	40	35	42	27	41	41	36
12	48	49	36	35	41	42	28	28	32	28	44	49	45	28	29	41	47	31	50	33
13	36	35	38	47	28	27	41	36	32	37	48	40	35	33	31	47	37	30	30	42
14	47	34	47	45	45	39	46	43	50	43	32	40	45	27	38	26	46	33	27	41
15	40	44	33	27	34	41	33	41	50	30	41	26	29	32	28	39	48	32	34	27
16	27	44	50	50	41	40	35	32	43	38	29	26	31	40	37	45	50	31	27	47
17	43	48	47	36	48	40	36	46	34	26	47	28	35	30	49	26	36	32	36	48
18	40	45	42	37	30	40	32	41	29	44	44	34	34	33	46	34	41	27	42	36
19	35	28	29	28	36	41	26	27	45	48	44	41	26	50	39	45	50	29	34	28
20	29	45	38	26	41	38	41	38	41	30	32	42	49	38	42	48	41	47	28	50
21	26	27	34	31	39	48	31	36	36	46	26	33	44	32	37	43	49	34	36	31
22	32	48	34	32	34	42	44	38	31	45	33	43	29	37	38	35	28	44	35	35
23	39	50	31	49	43	40	30	28	29	31	36	43	29	41	35	27	46	36	32	32
24	34	30	45	40	50	41	31	41	32	39	43	50	30	43	29	35	49	34	40	42
25	35	39	43	49	34	30	33	36	30	50	30	29	45	43	44	36	37	38	30	47
26	48	33	34	36	38	42	37	34	27	30	42	48	30	42	36	40	38	42	47	31
27	27	40	31	27	40	45	26	36	42	33	49	40	39	41	35	40	33	40	31	26
28	42	39	38	41	34	38	26	32	29	34	49	45	34	35	38	28	40	27	37	33
29	37	43	40	50	39	43	38	29	38	33	38	34	30	30	34	27	47	47	33	31
30	35	40	29	40	37	48	36	35	49	46	29	38	48	42	42	39	30	32	50	46
31	41	41	33	46	41	42	49	42	39	43	48	47	31	42	30	34	45	46	50	35
32	30	36	38	26	48	46	48	34	43	45	36	26	27	40	38	44	40	44	47	39
33	37	39	49	35	39	40	29	40	43	48	37	37	39	29	41	42	39	28	35	28
34	41	27	48	36	38	35	42	38	44	46	39	42	46	43	35	37	36	31	44	44
35	44	49	27	49	43	37	45	30	43	40	37	40	47	38	33	47	42	31	40	28
36	43	31	29	27	28	26	29	28	50	41	36	32	35	43	49	43	34	38	29	34
37	34	36	46	44	50	44	30	46	44	49	43	38	37	44	49	50	36	29	42	27
38	42	46	47	27	47	37	43	36	36	32	40	45	33	42	33	31	50	27	36	48
39	47	29	39	27	45	40	36	37	32	39	31	28	39	31	42	31	39	37	38	40
40	38	45	35	29	47	35	28	38	41	50	35	48	40	33	37	48	28	27	48	48
41	35	30	29	40	28	38	40	37	37	33	27	29	32	34	28	47	39	38	43	43
42	40	41	34	47	38	34	44	38	38	34	45	47	37	45	41	35	43	35	44	31
43	50	32	47	30	42	44	45	48	28	43	32	46	43	47	29	48	32	32	32	45
44	50	31	28	48	34	30	45	33	48	50	43	33	30	44	43	38	44	39	42	34
45	45	26	47	38	45	43	32	42	39	39	35	46	42	45	29	49	36	48	30	49
46	48	41	48	44	37	38	39	48	47	38	41	31	33	32	31	29	46	45	47	29
47	50	50	34	44	36	28	28	38	43	43	46	36	42	47	42	48	33	36	27	49
48	50	38	28	37	26	27	30	32	27	45	38	39	45	36	44	33	29	27	34	41
49	41	31	32	40	33	37	34	50	47	31	42	45	37	32	42	49	40	39	26	49
50	43	34	27	38	50	35	49	29	28	33	36	27	35	30	48	35	28	42	27	48

SAMPLE LABSTAT OUTPUT

```
joinder.dat    LABSTAT: Two-Factor Between-Subjects ANOVA      Page 1
**********************************************************************
```

Treatment Descriptives

Title: Joinder ANOVA Example

Dependent Variable: Verdict Rating

Factor A = Number Judged
Factor B = Number Filed

Factor A	Factor B	Cell	N	Mean	Std Dev	Std Err
One	One	1	10	3.800	1.229	0.389
One	Two	2	10	4.100	0.738	0.233
One	Three	3	10	4.300	0.949	0.300
One	Four	4	10	4.700	1.160	0.367
Two	One	5	10	4.400	0.966	0.306
Two	Two	6	10	4.400	0.843	0.267
Two	Three	7	10	4.800	0.789	0.249
Two	Four	8	10	5.200	0.632	0.200

Main Effects

Factor	Level	N	Mean	Std Dev	Std Err
Number Judged	One	40	4.225	1.050	0.166
	Two	40	4.700	0.853	0.135
Number Filed	One	20	4.100	1.119	0.250
	Two	20	4.250	0.786	0.176
	Three	20	4.550	0.887	0.198
	Four	20	4.950	0.945	0.211

Title: Joinder ANOVA Example

Dependent Variable: Verdict Rating

Source	SS	df	MS	F
Total	75.888	79		
Number Judged	4.513	1	4.513	5.182
Number Filed	8.438	3	2.813	3.230
A X B Inter	0.237	3	0.079	0.091
Error	62.700	72	0.871	

Name:	1J1F	1J2F	1J3F	1J4F
1	3.0000	5.0000	6.0000	2.0000
2	3.0000	4.0000	3.0000	4.0000
3	3.0000	4.0000	4.0000	5.0000
4	4.0000	4.0000	4.0000	5.0000
5	4.0000	5.0000	5.0000	5.0000
6	3.0000	3.0000	5.0000	5.0000
7	2.0000	3.0000	4.0000	5.0000
8	5.0000	4.0000	5.0000	4.0000
9	6.0000	4.0000	3.0000	6.0000
10	5.0000	5.0000	4.0000	6.0000

Name:	2J1F	2J2F	2J3F	2J4F
1	6.0000	3.0000	4.0000	5.0000
2	4.0000	5.0000	6.0000	5.0000
3	4.0000	5.0000	4.0000	5.0000
4	5.0000	5.0000	5.0000	6.0000
5	4.0000	4.0000	5.0000	5.0000
6	5.0000	5.0000	4.0000	4.0000
7	5.0000	4.0000	4.0000	5.0000
8	3.0000	5.0000	5.0000	5.0000
9	3.0000	5.0000	5.0000	6.0000
10	5.0000	3.0000	6.0000	6.0000

Treatment Descriptives

Title: Peterson & Peterson ANOVA Example

Dependent Variable: Recall

Factor A = Stimulus Type
Factor B = Retention Int.

Factor A	Factor B	Cell	N	Mean	Std Dev	Std Err
Words	3 sec	1	16	19.125	0.806	0.202
Words	18 sec	2	16	16.312	1.702	0.425
CCCs	3 sec	3	16	16.250	2.887	0.722
CCCs	18 sec	4	16	11.062	5.434	1.359

Main Effects

Factor	Level	N	Mean	Std Dev	Std Err
Stimulus Type	Words	32	17.719	1.938	0.343
	CCCs	32	13.656	5.026	0.889
Retention Int.	3 sec	32	17.687	2.546	0.450
	18 sec	32	13.687	4.775	0.844

Title: Peterson & Peterson ANOVA Example

Dependent Variable: Recall

Source	SS	df	MS	F
Total	1163.750	63		
Subjects	262.750	15		
Stimulus Type	264.063	1	264.063	16.577
Error A	238.937	15	15.929	
Retention Int.	256.000	1	256.000	64.000
Error B	60.000	15	4.000	
A X B Inter	22.562	1	22.562	5.694
Error A X B	59.437	15	3.962	

****
Name:	words/3sec	words/18sec	CCC/3sec	CCC/18sec
1	18.0000	16.0000	15.0000	15.0000
2	20.0000	17.0000	19.0000	18.0000
3	20.0000	13.0000	18.0000	14.0000
4	19.0000	18.0000	13.0000	4.0000
5	18.0000	16.0000	16.0000	11.0000
6	19.0000	17.0000	19.0000	17.0000
7	20.0000	15.0000	14.0000	7.0000
8	18.0000	15.0000	18.0000	7.0000
9	20.0000	19.0000	18.0000	15.0000
10	20.0000	18.0000	20.0000	17.0000
11	19.0000	14.0000	10.0000	5.0000
12	18.0000	16.0000	17.0000	16.0000
13	19.0000	15.0000	20.0000	16.0000
14	20.0000	16.0000	13.0000	3.0000
15	19.0000	19.0000	14.0000	6.0000
16	19.0000	17.0000	16.0000	6.0000

APPENDIX IV

STATISTICAL FORMULAS AND WORKED EXAMPLES

(I) Sum of Squares
(Gravetter & Wallnau, 1990)

$$SS = \sum X^2 - \frac{\left(\sum X\right)^2}{N}$$

Example:

X	X^2
3	9
5	25
8	64
9	81
6	36
2	4
$\sum = 33$	219

$$SS = 219 - \left(\frac{1089}{6}\right) = 37.5$$

(II) Standard Deviation (Using SS Formula)

$$S = \sqrt{\frac{SS}{(N-1)}}$$

$$\sigma = \sqrt{\frac{SS}{N}}$$

$$S = \sqrt{\frac{37.5}{5}} = 2.74$$

$$\sigma = \sqrt{\frac{37.5}{6}} = 2.50$$

(III) Pearson Correlation Coefficient
(Gravetter & Wallnau, 1990)

$$r = \frac{SP}{\sqrt{SS_x SS_y}}$$

where

$$SP = \sum XY - \frac{(\sum X)(\sum Y)}{N}$$

$$SS_x = \sum X^2 - \frac{(\sum X)^2}{N}$$

$$SS_y = \sum Y^2 - \frac{(\sum Y)^2}{N}$$

Example:

X	Y	$\sum XY$
6	5	30
4	6	24
6	7	42
7	9	63
5	4	20
$\sum = 28$	31	179

$$\sum X^2 = 162 \qquad \sum Y^2 = 207$$

$$SP = 179 - \frac{28 \times 31}{5} = 179 - 173.6 = 5.4$$

$$SS_x = 162 - \left(\frac{784}{5}\right) = 5.2$$

$$SS_y = 207 - \left(\frac{961}{5}\right) = 14.8$$

$$r = \frac{5.4}{\sqrt{(5.2)(14.8)}} = \frac{5.4}{8.77} = 0.62$$

(IV) Spearman Rank Order Correlation
(Gravetter & Wallnau, 1990)

$$r_s = \frac{SP}{\sqrt{SS_x SS_y}}$$

where

$$SP = \sum XY - \frac{(\sum X)(\sum Y)}{N}$$

SS_x and SS_y = the sums of squares for X and Y, respectively (see above for formula)

$\sum X$ and $\sum Y$ = the sums of the ranks for X and Y, respectively (see below)

Example:

X	Y	Rank X	Rank Y	XY
3	4	2	1	2
5	8	3	5	15
6	5	4	2	8
2	7	1	4	4
8	9	6	6	36
7	6	5	3	15
$\sum X$ and $\sum Y$		21	21	80
$\sum X^2$ and $\sum Y^2$		91	91	

$$SP = 80 - \frac{(21)(21)}{6} = 6.5$$

$$SS_x \text{ and } SS_y = 91 - \left(\frac{21^2}{6}\right) = 17.5$$

$$r_s = \frac{6.5}{\sqrt{(17.5)(17.5)}} = 0.37$$

(V) Point-Biserial Correlation
(Roscoe, 1975)

$$r_{pb} = \frac{M_1 - M_0}{\sigma_x} \sqrt{pq}$$

where

$\overline{X}_1$ = mean of the subjects on the continuous variable for subjects falling into Category 1 of the dichotomous variable

$\overline{X}_0$ = mean of the subjects on the continuous variable for subjects falling into Category 2 of the dichotomous variable

σ_x = standard deviation of the continuous variable

p = proportion of all subjects falling into Category 1

q = proportion of all subjects falling into Category 2

Example:

X	Y
6	1
7	1
5	0
4	0
8	1
2	0

$$\overline{X}_1 = \frac{6 + 7 + 8}{3} = 7$$

$$\overline{X}_0 = \frac{5 + 4 + 2}{3} = 3.67$$

$$\sigma_x = 1.97$$

$$p = 0.5$$

$$q = 0.5$$

$$r_{pb} = \frac{7 - 3.67}{1.97} \sqrt{(0.5)(0.5)} = 0.85$$

(VI) Partial Correlation
(Thorndike, 1978)

$$r_{12 \cdot 3} = \frac{r_{12} - r_{13}r_{23}}{\sqrt{1 - r_{13}^2} \; \sqrt{1 - r_{23}^2}}$$

Example:

$$r_{12} = 0.67$$

$$r_{13} = 0.55$$

$$r_{23} = 0.71$$

$$r_{12 \cdot 3} = \frac{(0.67 - [0.55][0.71])}{\sqrt{1 - 0.55^2} \; \sqrt{1 - 0.71^2}} = 0.47$$

(VII) Part Correlation (Semipartial Correlation)
(Thorndike, 1978)

$$r_{1(2 \cdot 3)} = \frac{r_{12} - r_{13}r_{23}}{\sqrt{1 - r_{23}^2}}$$

Example (using previous correlations):

$$r_{1(2 \cdot 3)} = \frac{.67 - (.55)(.71)}{\sqrt{1 - .72^2}} = .40$$

(VIII) One-Factor Between–Subjects ANOVA
(Keppel, 1982)

Preliminary Calculations

$$[A] = \frac{\sum Ai^2}{s} \qquad [T] = \frac{T^2}{as} \qquad [AS] = \sum (AS^2)$$

where

A_i = each treatment sum

T = total of all scores

s = number of subjects in each treatment group

a = number of levels of the independent variable

$\sum (AS)^2$ = sum of the squared scores

Calculation of Sum of Squares (SS), Degrees of Freedom (df), Mean Squares (MS), and F–ratio

$$SS_A = [A] - [T], \;\; SS_{S/A} = [AS] - [A]$$
$$df_A = (a - 1), \;\; df_{S/A} = a(s - 1)$$
$$MS_A = \frac{SS_A}{df_A}, \;\; MS_{S/A} = \frac{SS_{S/A}}{df_{S/A}}$$
$$F = \frac{MS_A}{MS_{S/A}}$$

Example:

	Group 1	Group 2	Group 3
	3	5	10
	2	6	9
	1	8	10
	3	7	9
	4	8	8
$\sum X$	13	34	46
$\sum X^2$	39	238	426
$\overline{X}$	2.6	6.8	9.2

$$[T] = \frac{(93)^2}{3(5)} = 576.6 \qquad [A] = \frac{(13)^2 + (34)^2 + (46)^2}{5} = 688.2$$

$$[AS] = (3)^2 + (2)^2 + \cdots + (9)^2 + (8)^2 = 703$$

$$SS_A = [A] - [T] = 688.2 - 576.6 = 111.6; \quad df_A = (3 - 1) = 2$$

$$SS_{S/A} = [AS] - [A] = 703 - 688.2 = 14.8; \quad df_{S/A} = 3(5 - 1) = 12$$

$$MS_A = \frac{111.6}{2} = 55.8$$

$$MS_{S/A} = \frac{14.8}{12} = 1.23$$

$$F_A = \frac{55.8}{1.23} = 45.36$$

(IX) One-Factor Within-Subjects ANOVA
(Keppel, 1982)

Preliminary Calculations

$$[A] = \frac{\sum A_i^2}{s}, \quad [T] = \frac{T^2}{as}, \quad [S] = \frac{\sum S_i^2}{a}, \quad [AS] = \sum (AS)^2$$

where

A_i = each treatment sum

s = number of subjects in each treatment group

T = total of all scores

a = number of levels of the independent variable

S_i = sum across levels of the independent variable for each subject

$\sum(AS)^2$ = sum of the squared scores

Calculation of Sum of Squares (SS), Degrees of Freedom (df), Mean Squares (MS), and F-ratio

$$SS_A = [A] - [T], \quad SS_S = [S] - [T], \quad SS_{AS} = [AS] - [A] - [S] + [T]$$

$$df_A = (a - 1), \quad df_S = (s - 1), \quad df_{AS} = (a - 1)(s - 1)$$

$$MS_A = \frac{SS_A}{df_A}, \quad MS_S = \frac{SS_S}{df_S}, \quad MS_{AS} = \frac{SS_{AS}}{df_{AS}}$$

$$F_A = \frac{MS_A}{MS_{AS}}, \quad F_S = \frac{MS_S}{MS_{AS}}$$

Example:

	Group 1	Group 2	Group 3	Sum
	3	5	10	18
	2	6	9	17
	1	8	10	19
	3	7	9	19
	4	8	8	20
$\sum X$	13	34	46	93
$\sum X^2$	39	238	426	
M	2.6	6.8	9.2	

$$[T] = \frac{(93)^2}{3(5)} = 576.6 \qquad [A] = \frac{(13)^2 + (34)^2 + (46)^2}{5} = 688.2$$

$$[S] = \frac{(18)^2 + (17)^2 + (19)^2 + (19)^2 + (20)^2}{3} = 578.33$$

$$[AS] = (3)^2 + (2)^2 + \cdots + (9)^2 + (8)^2 = 703$$

$$SS_A = [A] - [T] = 688.2 - 576.6 = 111.6; \quad df_A = (3 - 1) = 2$$

$$SS_S = [S] - [T] = 578.33 - 576.6 = 1.73; \quad df_S = (5 - 1) = 4$$

$$SS_{AS} = [AS] - [A] - [S] + [T] = 703 - 688.2 - 578.33 + 576.6$$
$$= 13.07; \quad df_{AS} = (3 - 1)(5 - 1) = 8$$

$$MS_A = \frac{111.6}{2} = 55.8$$

$$MS_S = \frac{1.73}{4} = 0.44$$

$$MS_{AS} = \frac{13.07}{8} = 1.63$$

$$F_A = \frac{55.8}{1.63} = 34.23$$

$$F_S = \frac{0.44}{1.63} < 1$$

(X) Two-Factor Between-Subjects ANOVA
(Keppel, 1982)

Preliminary Calculations

$$[A] = \frac{\sum A_i^2}{bs}, \quad [B] = \frac{\sum B_i^2}{as}, \quad [AB] = \frac{\sum (AB_{ij})^2}{s},$$

$$[T] = \frac{T^2}{abs}, \quad [ABS] = \sum (ABS)^2$$

where

a = number of levels of Factor a

b = number of levels of Factor b

s = number of subjects per group

A_i = each treatment sum for Factor A

B_j = each treatment sum for Factor B

AB_{ij} = sum of the scores in each cell

s = number of subjects in each group

T = total of all scores

$\sum (ABS)^2$ = sum of the squared scores

Calculation of Sum of Squares (SS), Degrees of Freedom (df), Mean Squares (MS), and F-ratio

$$SS_A = [A] - [T], \quad SS_B = [B] - [T],$$

$$SS_{AB} = [AB] - [A] - [B] + [T], \quad SS_{S/AB} = [ABS] - [AB]$$

$$df_A = (a - 1), \quad df_B = (b - 1), \quad df_{AB} = (a - 1)(b - 1), \quad df_{S/AB} = ab(s - 1)$$

$$MS_A = \frac{SS_A}{df_A}, \quad MS_B = \frac{SS_B}{df_B}, \quad MS_{AB} = \frac{SS_{AB}}{df_{AB}}, \quad MS_{S/AB} = \frac{SS_{S/AB}}{df_{S/AB}}$$

$$F_A = \frac{MS_A}{MS_{S/AB}}, \quad F_B = \frac{MS_B}{MS_{S/AB}}, \quad F_{AB} = \frac{MS_{AB}}{MS_{S/AB}}$$

Example:

	A_1		A_2	
	B_1	B_2	B_1	B_2
	2	1	3	10
	3	2	3	10
	0	1	2	9
	1	5	1	9
	4	3	4	10
$\sum X =$	10	12	13	48
$\sum X^2 =$	30	40	39	462
$M =$	2	2.4	2.6	9.6

$$[T] = \frac{(83)^2}{(2)(2)(5)} = 344.45 \qquad [A] = \frac{(22)^2 + (61)^2}{2(5)} = 420.5$$

$$[B] = \frac{(23)^2 + (60)^2}{2(5)} = 412.9$$

$$[AB] = \frac{(10)^2 + (13)^2 + (12)^2 + (48)^2}{5} = 543.4$$

$$[ABS] = (2)^2 + (3)^2 + \cdots + (9)^2 + (10)^2 = 571$$

$$SS_A = [A] - [T] = 420.5 - 344.45 = 76.05; \quad df_A = (2 - 1) = 1$$

$$SS_B = [B] - [T] = 412.9 - 344.45 = 68.45; \quad df_B = (2 - 1) = 1$$

$$SS_{AB} = [AB] - [A] - [B] + [T] = 543.4 - 420.5 - 412.9 + 344.5 = 54.5$$

$$df_{AB} = (2 - 1)(2 - 1) = 1$$

$$SS_{S/AB} = [ABS] - [AB] = 571 - 543.4 = 27.6$$

$$df_{S/AB} = (2)(2)(5 - 1) = 16$$

$$MS_A = \frac{76.05}{1} = 76.05 \qquad F_A = 43.96$$

$$MS_B = \frac{68.45}{1} = 68.45 \qquad F_B = 39.56$$

$$MS_{AB} = \frac{54.5}{1} = 54.5 \qquad F_{AB} = 31.5$$

$$MS_{S/AB} = \frac{27.6}{16} = 1.73$$

(XI) z Test for Two Proportions
(Glassnap & Poggio, 1985)

$$z = \frac{P_1 - P_2}{\sqrt{P_p(1 - P_p)\left(\frac{1}{n_1} + \frac{1}{n_2}\right)}}$$

where

P_1 and P_2 = the two proportions

n_1 and n_2 = number of subjects in each group

P_p = a calculation from the observed frequency (f) in each group with the following formula:

$$P_p = \frac{f_1 + f_2}{n_1 + n_2}$$

where

f_1 = frequency of the observed response in Group 1

f_2 = frequency of the observed response in Group 2

n_1 and n_2 = number of subjects in each group

Example:

$$P_1 = 0.80$$

$$P_2 = 0.30$$

$$n_1 = n_2 = 10$$

$$P_p = \frac{(8 + 3)}{(10 + 10)} = 0.55$$

$$z = \frac{(0.8 - 0.3)}{\sqrt{0.55(1 - 0.55)\left(\frac{1}{10} + \frac{1}{10}\right)}} = 2.24$$

(XII) Formula for Squared Semipartial Correlation
(Tabachnik & Fidell, 1989)

$$sr_i^2 = \frac{F}{df_{residual}} (1 - R^2)$$

Note: If the program you are using provides *t* values rather than *F*-ratios, simply square *t* (t^2) and substitute that value for *F* in the formula.

(XIII) Chi-square for a Two-Way Contingency Table
(Roscoe, 1975)

$$\chi^2 = \sum \frac{(O_{ij} - E_{ij})^2}{E_{ij}}$$

where

O_{ij} = observed frequency within a cell

E_{ij} = expected frequency within a cell, defined as

$$E_{ij} = \frac{R_i \times C_j}{N}$$

where

R_i = the appropriate row sum

C_j = the appropriate column sum

N = the total frequency count over all cells

Example:

Table of Observed Frequencies

	C_1	C_2	Row Sum
R_1	25	12	37
R_2	14	35	49
Column Sum	39	47	86

Expected Frequencies:

$$E_{1,1} = \frac{39 \times 37}{86} = 16.8$$

$$E_{1,2} = \frac{47 \times 37}{86} = 20.2$$

$$E_{2,1} = \frac{39 \times 49}{86} = 22.2$$

$$E_{2,2} = \frac{47 \times 49}{86} = 26.8$$

$$\chi^2 = \frac{(25 - 16.8)^2}{16.8} + \frac{(12 - 20.2)^2}{20.2} + \frac{(14 - 22.2)^2}{22.2} + \frac{(35 - 26.8)^2}{26.8} = 12.87$$

(XIV) Mann–Whitney U test
(Roscoe, 1975)

$$U_a = n_a n_b + \frac{n_b(n_b + 1)}{2} - \sum R_b$$

$$U_b = n_a n_b + \frac{n_a(n_a + 1)}{2} - \sum R_a$$

where

n_a = the number of subjects in Group a

n_b = the number of subjects in Group b

R_a and R_b are the sums of the ranks for Groups a and b, respectively

Example:

Group a	Group b
23	14
32	21
15	33
39	18
22	16

Distribution of Ordered Scores

Scores and (group)	Rank	Group a Ranks	Group b Ranks
14 (b)	1		1
15 (a)	2	2	
16 (b)	3		3
18 (b)	4		4
21 (b)	5		5
22 (a)	6	6	
23 (a)	7	7	
32 (a)	8	8	
33 (b)	9		9
39 (a)	10	10	
Sum of Ranks		33	22

$n_a = 5$
$n_b = 5$

$$U_a = 5 \times 5 + \frac{5(5 + 1)}{2} - 22 = 18$$

$$U_b = 5 \times 5 + \frac{5(5 + 1)}{2} - 33 = 7$$

(XV) t test for Independent Samples

$$t = \frac{\overline{X}_t - \overline{X}_c}{S_{\overline{X}_t - \overline{X}_c}}$$

where

$\overline{X}_t$ = mean for the group receiving the treatment

$\overline{X}_c$ = mean for the control group

$S_{\overline{X}_t - \overline{X}_c}$ = the standard error defined as:

$$S_{\overline{X}_t - \overline{X}_c} = \sqrt{\frac{SS_t + SS_c}{(n_t + n_c) - 2}\left(\frac{1}{n_t} + \frac{1}{n_c}\right)}$$

Example:

Treatment (t)	Control (c)
9	3
8	2
7	2
7	1
6	3
8	4
9	2
10	1
7	5
8	3
$\overline{X}$ = 7.9	2.6

$$S_{\overline{X}_t - \overline{X}_c} = \sqrt{\frac{12.6 + 14.4}{(10 + 10) - 2}\left(\frac{1}{10} + \frac{1}{10}\right)} = .551$$

$$t = \frac{7.9 - 2.6}{.551} = 9.62$$

(XVI) t test for Correlated Samples

Roscoe (1975)

$$t = \frac{\overline{D}}{S_{\overline{D}}}$$

where

$\overline{D}$ = the average of the difference scores between pairs of scores (treatment − control). In the equations that follow, "D" refers to a difference score.

$S_{\overline{D}}$ = the standard error of d defined as:

$$S_{\overline{D}} = \sqrt{\frac{\Sigma d^2}{N(N-1)}}$$

where

$$\Sigma d^2 = \Sigma D^2 - \frac{(\Sigma D)^2}{N}$$

Example:

Treatment (t)	Control (c)	D	D²
9	3	6	36
8	2	6	36
7	2	5	25
7	1	6	36
6	3	3	9
8	4	4	16
9	2	7	49
10	1	9	81
7	5	2	4
8	3	5	25

$$\Sigma D = 53 \qquad \Sigma D_2 = 317$$
$$\overline{D} = 5.3$$

$$\Sigma d^2 = 317 - \frac{53^2}{10} = 36.1$$

$$S_{\overline{D}} = \sqrt{\frac{36.1}{10(9)}} = .633$$

$$t = \frac{5.3}{.633} = 8.37$$